An Account of the Cruise of the St. George on the North American and West Indian Station

Nicholas Belfield Dennys

BIBLIOLIFE

AN ACCOUNT

OF THE

CRUISE OF THE ST. GEORGE

ON

THE NORTH AMERICAN AND WEST INDIAN STATION.

During the Years 1861–1862.

By N. B. DENNYS,

ASSISTANT PAYMASTER, R.N.

LONDON:

SAUNDERS, OTLEY, AND CO.,

66, BROOK STREET, HANOVER SQUARE.

1862.

TO

THE OFFICERS OF THE ST. GEORGE,

THE FOLLOWING PAGES,

DESCRIPTIVE OF OUR TOUR IN NORTH AMERICA AND THE

WEST INDIES,

ARE DEDICATED, IN MEMORY OF MANY PLEASANT HOURS

PASSED IN THEIR SOCIETY,

BY THE AUTHOR.

CONTENTS.

CHAPTER I.

OUTWARD-BOUND—BARBADOES 1

CHAPTER II.

ST. VINCENT AND ST. LUCIA 21

CHAPTER III.

MARTINIQUE TO ANTIGUA 36

CHAPTER IV.

MONTSERRAT TO SANTA CRUZ 58

CHAPTER V.

PORT ROYAL—JAMAICA 73

CHAPTER VI.

KINGSTON—JAMAICA 89

CHAPTER VII.

GREAT INAGUA, LONG ISLAND. BERMUDA . . . 109

CHAPTER VIII.

HALIFAX 119

CHAPTER IX.

ᴘᴀɢᴇ

ARICHAT AND LOUISBURG TO SYDNEY 132

CHAPTER X.

HALIFAX.—BALLS AND THEATRICALS 146

CHAPTER XI.

HALIFAX—AMUSEMENTS—SOCIETY, ETC. 162

CHAPTER XII.

NOVA SCOTIA GOLDFIELDS.—SYDNEY 173

CHAPTER XIII.

THE BAHAMAS 190

CHAPTER XIV.

PORT ROYAL TO CAPE SAN ANTONIO 215

CHAPTER XV.

VERA CRUZ AND ANTON LIZARDO 227

CHAPTER XVI.

THE HAVANA 243

CHAPTER XVII.

BERMÚDA.—HOME—CONCLUSION 261

LIST OF PLACES VISITED BY H.M.S. ST. GEORGE, WITH
DATES OF ARRIVAL AND DEPARTURE 266

INTRODUCTION.

THE following pages consist mainly of extracts from a private journal kept by me during the cruise of Her Majesty's Ship *St. George*, on the North American and West Indian station.

Some apology seems due for thus venturing to bring them before the public, but as its estimation of them will be but little affected by any I can offer, I will not undertake to excuse either the fact of its publication, or the many faults and shortcomings which it doubtless contains.

On one or two subjects I would, however, offer a remark. It will be easily understood that it is extremely difficult, in a work of this description, to avoid a frequent use of the first personal pronoun; and a knowledge of this will, I trust, save me from the imputation of egotism, on account of the number of times the phrase " *I* did or saw this or that," occurs.

The extracts from the colonial press have been, in many cases, given at great length, because, in addition to their describing better than I could the proceedings at the various places visited, they serve to illustrate the tone of society, and the general feelings of loyalty which universally characterize our transatlantic colonies.

It may be urged that the same ground has before this been gone over, and well described by those who have given to the world the results of their observations. True—but they did not belong to the *St. George*.

It is hoped that my readers will distinctly understand that the impressions herein recorded are my own, and not those of others belonging to the ship; and that for all opinions set forth, I alone am responsible.

A gentleman, whose opinion I much value, has reminded me that the feelings of the people we have visited should be respected. I have, I trust, said nothing which may in any way offend those to whose hospitality we were so much indebted; but, at the same time, have not hesitated to speak what I believe to be the truth. If I have been inclined to look too much on the ludicrous aspect presented by the society we have mixed with, it

will, I trust, forgive me.   There can be little malice
where there is much laughter.

My best thanks are due to those who have so
kindly aided me by sketches and notes.   It would
be invidious to particularize individuals, where so
many have aided.

In conclusion, I would only add, that I trust the
perusal of the following pages will recall to the
minds of my shipmates many pleasant hours spent
among the scenes mentioned therein.

N. B. D.

H.M. Ship *St. George*,
   May 9th, 1862.

THE CRUISE

OF

H.M. SHIP "ST. GEORGE."

***

CHAPTER I.

OUTWARD-BOUND——BARBADOES.

"The open sea,
I am where I would ever be."—*The Sea.*

IT has often been a matter of speculation to me
whether the author of the above lines ever under-
went that soul-and-body-parting malady sea-sick-
ness. I should rather fancy that he was a total
stranger to the sufferings endured by those who,
less fortunate, are obliged to make periodical tours
to the ship's side, to ease their minds and stomachs
by "feeding the fishes." Being myself a constant
victim to this distressing but necessary performance,
I most unequivocally protest against the sentiments
contained in the song above quoted from, feeling
assured that I shall have the sympathy of a large
proportion of those, who, although brother-officers
(and therefore supposed to be accustomed to the
combination of perpendicular, horizontal, and lateral

B

motion which characterizes the movement of a ship
in a heavy sea), seldom leave port without experi-
encing a sort of qualmish inconvenience in exchanging the quietude of a snug anchorage for the disagreeable motion aforesaid.

Such, at all events, were my reflections about the
17th and 18th of January, 1861, having left Plymouth in Her Majesty's ship *St. George*, (on board
which His Royal Highness Prince Alfred was
embarked as midshipman,) on the 15th of that
month, bound on a cruise to the West Indies and
Spanish Main.

I have often wondered how many descriptions of
gales of wind have at various times been written or
published. The subject is truly a stale one; but as
the following pages profess to give an account, "full,
true, and particular," of our cruise, I shall make no
apology for again describing a scene familiar enough
to all naval men.

For the first few days after leaving Plymouth,
the weather was, though not pleasant, only breezy,
and favourable to our course. We therefore soon
cleared the Channel, and, like misguided mortals as
we were, indulged in sanguine hopes of a quick
passage to Barbadoes—the first island we were to
visit. Our anticipations were doomed to be disappointed, for on the 19th the wind headed us, the
ship began to knock about in the most uncomfort-
able manner, and our harbour luxuries of milk,

fresh vegetables, &c., having run out, we began to experience the usual delights of a cruise in the North Atlantic off the British coast, in the month of January. Strange to say, however, although we mustered pretty strong in the mess, in spite of a generally-prevailing qualmishness, no one seemed inclined to forego his share of the meals; but manfully endorsed the nautical opinion that, under such circumstances, the more one eats the better they'll be for it.

I have met very few men who liked the sea *per se*. Undoubtedly most naval men are proud of their profession, but at the same time prefer smooth water to rough. No doubt regular old salts take a delight, like the celebrated Billy Bowline, in riding " o'er the salt sea foam;" but the new school, I fancy, have a more vivid appreciation of the comforts of a snug anchorage.

Any individual who really *does* take a delight in the eternal knocking about one gets in a heavy sea with a head wind, might have taken passage in the *St. George* on this occasion with advantage to himself, as far as his tastes in that way were concerned. The wind increased in strength till the 24th or 25th January. On the evening of the latter day the barometer fell still lower than previously, and night closed in with as unpleasant a promise of a hard blow as I ever recollect to have seen. About eleven, p.m., the gale reached its height, and the

scene to any one who could so far overcome his
sense of discomfort as to view it in an artistic point
of view, was magnificent in the extreme. A close-
reefed main-topsail was almost the only canvas we
could show to the gale, and that we expected every
moment would be blown away. The ship heeled
over to an angle of thirty degrees, and took in seas
over her bows and waist continuously. The upper,
main, and lower decks were all afloat, and the orlop
(in which the chests of the gun-room officers were
billeted) had on it from twelve to twenty inches of
water. Squall followed squall in quick succession,
and she occasionally rolled so heavily that the
chests aforesaid, scorning to be detained in their
places by cleats or lashings, dashed wildly from side
to side of the cockpit, performing acrobatic feats to
which those mentioned in the " Cornhill Magazine"
article on Spirit-rapping were but mere ordinary
occurrences. Of course the contents of those which
were not water-tight (and that unfortunately included the greater number of them) got soaked in a
way anything but satisfactory to their owners.

   In the mess-room, crockery was smashed, books
and instruments came to " grief," and altogether,
when daylight broke next morning, we presented
the most dreary aspect of discomfort imaginable.

   A gale of wind forms a capital study for the
artist, and is an interesting picture in an illustrated
paper; but there is a stern reality about it when

one meets it at sea which I must confess *I* don't by any means appreciate.

The next morning, the force of the gale broke, but extremely dirty weather was yet in store for us. A poor fellow fell overboard this afternoon. Our captain's coxswain gallantly jumped after him, though a very heavy sea was running at the time. He was too late to render him any assistance, as he sank at the moment of falling overboard. Our lifeboat, which was immediately manned, fortunately picked up the coxswain and returned with him to the ship in safety.

Again the wind freshened till it became a gale, and for two or three days we had another edition of the scene just described. At the end of that time we went about to the northward, and shortly afterwards caught a fair wind, which put us well on our course to Barbadoes, where we arrived on the 21st February, 1861, no incident of any moment having happened since we bid farewell to bad weather.

We found the ship to be an excellent sea-boat, but by some oversight the "authorities" appear to have run short of pitch and oakum when caulking her—at least, I suppose they did, for to use Jack's emphatic language, "She leaked like the very d—." No doubt the straining had a good deal to do with it, so we wont set down too much to the account of the dockyard artificers.

We anchored on arrival in Carlisle Bay, where we found Her Majesty's ships *Nile, Styx,* and *Barracouta.* From the days when Marryat wrote his "Peter Simple" to the present‾ time, Carlisle Bay has formed a favourite peg on which to hang a description; but I must confess that there does not appear to me to be anything particularly picturesque in this well-known harbour. A great want of taste, doubtless; but I must refer any one who wants a glowing description of it to the pages of the great naval novelist.

Now, if I were writing a guide-book, I suppose the following would be about the style of beginning :—

"Barbadoes is the easternmost island of the windward West Indian group, and lies in the path of the trade-winds, which are constantly blowing," &c. ; but as I presume no one will turn over these pages to look for information which any geographical work or sailing-directions will supply, I shall not proceed further in my quotation from one of those works, but "turn ahead" at once, and proceed with our own particular doings.

As the daily papers of Barbadoes supplied the fullest information of the doings of His Royal Highness, I cannot do better than make an extract from one of them entire, which will give a general sketch of the reception he met from the loyal inhabitants of Barbadoes.

"Once more has our little island been favoured

with the presence of a scion of the Royal Family, a
Prince of the blood royal, whose visit has been so
joyously looked forward to during the last three
weeks, that our inhabitants have not had time to
think of anything else. Nothing could exceed the
pleasurable feelings which animated all, from the
highest to the lowest, at this anticipated visit,
except the actual realization of the honour proposed : it was a sailor Prince who last visited us,
and it is a sailor Prince who now treads on our
shores, and who besides is the son of our Most
Gracious Majesty Queen Victoria, more beloved by
her subjects than any queen that ever ascended the
throne of Great Britain. We, in common with the
loyal inhabitants of this our island home, tender to
His Royal Highness Prince Alfred the homage
due unto his name, and firmly believe that he will
be a bright star in the profession he has chosen,
which has nurtured and brought up so many heroes
as examples for all our naval officers to follow.
But our space is brief and our record long, so to
our subject.

" At five p.m. on Thursday, a signal was made at
Moncrieff of a ship to windward ; shortly after it
was made a man-of-war, and then a ship of the
line, which ultimately proved to be the *St. George*.
The Harbour-Master boarded the ship outside the
bay, returning a little after ten o'clock, bringing
the welcome intelligence that the Prince was on

board and in good health.   Captain Beresford, Aide-
de-Camp to His Excellency the Governor, soon after
went on board to Major Cowell, who informed him
that he would visit the Governor the following day,
in order to make arrangements for the landing of
His Royal Highness in state on the Saturday.   On
Friday morning, the Union Jack was hoisted at all
the signal stations throughout the island, so that
all might know the joyous news of the Prince's safe
arrival; workmen were engaged decorating the
public and private arches in town, and giving
the last finishing touches to the platforms and
stands erected for the occasion; flags were hoisted
by all who had them, and pleasure, not business,
seemed to be the order of the day—a holiday they
were ordered by proclamation to keep, and a holiday they were determined to keep.   Advertisements appeared in the papers from the Aide-de-Camp
in waiting, stating that the landing would take
place at half-past ten a.m. on Saturday; that on the
arrival of the Prince at Government House a *levee*
would be held immediately; that the *déjeuner*
would take place at five p.m., and a display of fireworks at eight p.m.; but that the ball at Government
House in honour of His Royal Highness Prince
Alfred would not take place until Monday evening,
in consequence of the following day being Sunday.
With such a bill of fare of enjoyment and pleasure
before them, the god Morpheus was early sought

for, and we may safely assert, that he watched over
fewer sorrowful hearts or aching heads that night
than ever he had done before in Barbadoes. By
daybreak the next morning, people were seen hur-
rying in from the country by hundreds. The
Yeomanry Cavalry ordered for duty that day, as
also the police, were coming in from all parts of the
island, and persons as early as seven o'clock were
taking possession of their seats to enable them to
have a good view of the sailor son of the Queen."

Then follows an account of the procession, which
is a matter of mere local interest. After wading
through the list of persons presented, we next come
to an account of the *déjeuner*.

"Soon after four o'clock, some 240 gentlemen, comprising every one in the island who was entitled to
claim the honour of meeting His Royal Highness
at Government House, were assembled in the ball-
room, and shortly after the appointed hour descended to the grand new dining saloon, erected
expressly for the joyous occasion, and took their
seats around tables extending in length to nearly
one hundred yards, superbly decorated, and sump-
tuously furnished with every *viande* which zeal,
taste, and wealth could procure, or that an Epicurus
could fancy. Justice having been done to the
banquet before them, His Excellency the Governor-
General rose to propose the health of Her Most
Gracious Majesty the Queen. His Excellency

stated that during the evening he would only give
three toasts ; and that as he felt it utterly unneces-
sary to stimulate the loyalty of those assembled on
this festive occasion, he would propose the first
toast without any speech or preface.

"His Excellency was quite right in his estimation of Barbadoes loyalty, for never was a toast
drunk with more heartfelt enthusiasm than that of
— *The Queen.*

" The second toast proposed by his Excellency
was the health of the Prince Consort, of Prince
Albert, and the rest of the Royal Family—
which was drunk with nine times nine hearty
cheers.

"His Excellency then rose to propose a toast,
which he said he would endeavour to give without
making a speech, although it was impossible for
him to prevent himself from remarking 'that the
name he was about to announce to them was one
dear to every British heart.   It was owned by one
who was second son of our Gracious Queen, by one
who had chosen for his profession that in which a
Rodney and a Nelson had won eternal laurels—a
profession in which the British Colonies held a
peculiar interest, as the Navy was their bulwark
and the protection of their dearest hopes.   His
Excellency then alluded in flattering terms to the
feeling of the Barbadians towards the sister service,
and returning to the subject of his toast, most

happily set forth the fact, that the people of this
colony had welcomed His Royal Highness Prince
Alfred to their shores with the most heartfelt
loyalty, as the son of their Queen, but that those
who had since the good fortune to make His Royal
Highness's acquaintance, would, for his own sake,
hail his visit to them with tenfold enthusiasm.

"His Excellency concluded a brief but most
feeling and telling speech (during the delivery of
which he was frequently interrupted by bursts of
applause), by proposing the health of His Royal
Highness Prince Alfred, the guest of the Island of
Barbadoes.

"We shall not attempt to describe the manner
in which the announcement of the toast was received—enough to say, that longer, louder, or more
enthusiastic cheering was never heard within the
walls of Government House.

"At eight o'clock the company adjourned to the
galleries and porch commanding a view of the
stage, from which were to be exhibited the grand
display of fireworks which were to be let off in
honour of the occasion.

"At about a quarter past eight the first rocket
was exploded, and for over two hours every sort of
combustible was fired, exploded, ascending and de-
scending—and sending its brilliancy around to the
delight of thousands of interested and highly
pleased spectators, who eventually dispersed in the

best good order—all giving ninety-nine cheers for Prince Alfred.

"And so ended a day which broke without cloud —closed without a cloud—and will ever be noted in the annals of Barbadoes as the brightest on its historic page."

A true born Barbadian—a white man—is called a "Bim." Whence this uneuphonic name arose I cannot say, but it is not by any means a pretty one. Some individual raved in the "Barbadoes Globe" about "The flower of Bim's loveliness blooming again." As I fancy my readers will laugh over them as much as I did, I quote them below :

> " I've seen Alfred, too, the handsome tar of *George's* crew,
>   Smiling his greetings on thousands that waved,
> In sunny land of joy, with no cold allow,
>   And ne'er by such loveliness was he enslaved.
> I've seen the meeting of beauty, beauty greeting,
>   Gatherins (*sic*) of lasses in ball-room and plane (*sic*),
> But ne'er was beholden (*sic*) such sight by young or olden,
>   As the flower of Bim's loveliness blooming again."

On Monday, the 20th, the Governor gave a grand ball, to which the *élite* of the island were invited ; about nine of us went. I must confess that the said *élite* appears to comprehend an indefinite amount of colonial society. But perhaps my views on this subject are peculiar. The fair sex, however, will not I trust feel offended if I direct the attention of speculators in perfumery to the fact, that an importation of eau de Cologne, superior in

quality to that now in use at Barbadoes, would be
conferring a public benefit on its inhabitants.

On Wednesday, a ball was given by the merchants
of the island.   It took place in the upper story of
a large factory, and was extremely well got up, and
the general arrangements reflected great credit on
the stewards and managers.

On Thursday, the General gave *his* ball. Rather
quick work this, three balls in four days.   And
everybody who went to them meant dancing too,
and no mistake.   Talk about English girls dancing !
I'll back Creole young ladies against them any day,
as far as powers of endurance go.

After devoting so many lines to the whites of
Barbaboes, it is but fair now to give the blacks a
chance. The first with whom we made any acquaintance were the washerwomen. They are of all colours
and ages, and certainly never lose custom for want
of asking for it.   On the present occasion they had
two objects in view : one of which was to get
one's dirty clothes—the other, to see the Prince.
Of course to be slobbered over by a lot of females
(even white ones) is an extremely disagreeable operation to undergo at any time ; but no amount of
good nature could stand twenty black ones ; so the
honours were divided, each of the younger members
of the mess being pointed out in turn as " de Prince
his-self."   Great was their indignation when they
found out, one after another, how they had been

sold. A great amount of chaff took place occasionally with them, which sometimes ended in their
leaving the mess in a rage; though I must confess
that they would stand an immense amount before
they lost their temper.

One evening, one of these women, " Miss Jane
Anne Smith," gave a dignity ball. Now Jane
Anne stands about six feet one inch in her slippers,
and felt conscious of an even more imposing altitude
because she had the Prince's washing—a fact which
she did not fail to impress upon her rivals for that
honour in a way which did *not* produce a retort
courteous. So when Jane Anne issued the following card—

> Miss Jane Anne Smith *will be*
> *happy of your company to a dignity*
> *ball this evening in Chelsea Road.*
>
> *Thursday, Feb. 28th.*

we, in consideration of her connexion with royalty,
promised to go.

I am afraid all who promised did not keep their
word. However, I and a few others went, and
must say that, after what we had read and heard of
these affairs, we were somewhat disappointed. It
was given in a middling-sized room, with open
lattices, surrounded by a verandah in which coloured
lanterns were hanging. Some of the dark beauties (?)

were very well got up. Silks and muslin, jewellery, white satin shoes, and even white kid gloves, were to be seen. One sable party, who had scented her handkerchief, &c., in the most liberal way, had omitted to perform the same operation on her wool, which, having been plentifully doused with cocoa-nut oil, emitted an anything but pleasing fragrance; added to which she had no gloves, and possessed the clammy hands and unmistakeable *black* odour which invariably accompanies a coloured individual in the tropics. So that on the whole a very little of her company went a very long way. I came away about half-past ten, Miss Jane Anne demanding "someting for de dignity" before I left.

There is a capital ice-house in Bridgetown, kept by an American. The yearly consumption is said to equal 1000 tons. People at home don't know the blessings of such an institution, or the extensive patronage such a place enjoys. Our first inquiry at any place we visited in the tropics was always, "Is there an ice-house here?" and great was our grief when we learnt that some of the islands had not yet arrived at such a pitch of civilization as to support one.

Barbadoes appears to be in a high state of cultivation. Sugar-cane plantations burst into view at every opening between the houses on the roads leading to the capital. The sugar-mills seem rather obsolete pieces of machinery, being generally windmills; but are, I suppose, like the cabby's horse, " rum uns to look at, but *stunners* to go." The mechanical arrangements seem very simple ; but I had no opportunity of examining their interiors, all of them being closed in consequence of the blacks having all gone to " welcome de Prince," a proceeding which apparently occupied them some two or three days.

Towards the right hand or eastern side of the bay there is a pretty good watering-place. The ground is here free from sharks, being protected by a reef, and is therefore safe to bathe in. On the left side of the bay is situated the slaughter-house, which is of course always surrounded by sharks, as they frequent it for the offal, &c., thrown into the water, the building being erected on piles below low-water mark. The barracks are apparently very pleasantly situated in the midst of foliage, and beyond them again the spire of the cathedral is visible. A great number of English and American ships were at anchor in the bay on our arrival, and being all dressed in flags, gave it a very animated appearance. The weather has, for the West Indies, been pretty cool. As to the brave 'Badians themselves, or rather the coloured population, I am afraid their morality is not of the highest order. One thing, however, I cannot help noticing, and that is, the very superior intelligence of the Quadroons and Mulattoes generally to any I have hitherto met.

A strong proof, I imagine, that the black race are not by any means, as some assert, incapable of improvement and education. Of course, in the half-breeds, the admixture of white blood would, in a great degree, account for it; but the thorough " darkies " seem fairly intelligent. The children, too, seem more knowing than whites of the same age.

There is no intermixture between the whites and blacks, and the latter are never admitted into white society. One or two coloured clergymen and lawyers are, I believe, the almost sole exceptions to this rule, and even their presence at balls was the subject of much remark (the reverse of complimentary) by the ladies I happened to converse with during our stay at Barbadoes.

I cannot take leave of this independent little island without acknowledging the universal hospitality we experienced from its inhabitants. All vied in attentions and civilities. So may Barbadoes flourish and prosper. We left Carlisle Bay at five, p.m., on the 1st of March, 1861.

NOTES ON CHAPTER I.

ALTHOUGH it is my intention in the body of this little work to refrain as much as possible from introducing statements or information which may be met with in books previously published, yet, as I imagine that a few particulars of the history, products, and geology of the places visited may be useful to those

C

who may be unable to consult the original authorities, it is my intention to embody in the notes a few remarks on these subjects. The following are some of my authorities : — Somerville's "Physical Geography," Martin's "British Colonies," Trollope's "West Indies and Spanish Main," Brun's "History of St. Lucia," Colridge's "Six Months in the West Indies," &c., &c. To. W. Montgomery Martin's work I am deeply indebted, and I should strongly recommend any one about to pass any time in the West Indies, to provide himself with a copy of that work.

Barbadoes is about 21 miles long by 12 in breadth ; circumference 55 miles or thereabouts ; superficial area 106,470 acres, or about 166 square miles. Its general measurements approximate to those of the Isle of Wight.

It is supposed to have been discovered in 1518. Its name is attributed to the Portuguese, who, in their voyages to Brazil, are conjectured to be the first Europeans who landed here. They called it Las Barbadas or Barbados, signifying "long beard," in allusion to the abundance of a species of fig-tree, the *Ficus laurifolia*, from whose branches masses of twisted fibrous roots hang downwards like luxuriant beards.

The highest elevation in the island is Mount Hillaby, which is 1147 feet above the sea. The coast-line affords no harbours. The largest river is called Scotland River, whose waters being carried on their exit to the sea, expand into a basin called Long Pond. Water is obtained by sinking wells, of which there exist nearly 500 on the island. There are a few chalybeate springs containing chiefly iron, carbonic acid, and fixed alkali in different proportions. The boiling spring, one of the great natural curiosities of the island, consists of an inflammable gas (carburetted hydrogen), which issues from a spot about two feet in diameter near the side of a watercourse at Turner's Hall Wood, in St. Andrew's parish. On being lighted, the gas burns with a pure whitish light.

The situation of Bridgetown, though convenient, is insalubrious from its contiguity to a large swamp, which is, however, in process of being drained by convict labour.

Freemasonry flourishes greatly in Barbadoes. There are three or four lodges. Hastings and Worthing are two favourite watering-places on the coast. The other three towns are named

James or *Hole Town*, *Spikes Town*, and *Oistin* (named after an early settler), which, however, now contains only a few houses in a very dilapidated condition.

The products of the island at the present day comprise little beyond sugar, molasses, and rum. Cotton and coffee were at one time largely exported, but are not now considered among the principal exports.

There are, I believe, four or five bi-weekly papers. In 1851 the census was 135,939, of which 15,824 were whites. The births annually greatly exceed the deaths. There is a bishopric at Barbadoes; the diocese includes the leeward islands.

Geology.—The foundations consist of step-formed coral terraces. This structure exhibits two distinct features—1st. Coralline limestone with beds of calcareous marl containing recent shells; and 2nd. Strata of silicious sandstone, intermixed with ferruginous matter, calcareous sandstone, silicious limestone, different kinds of clay, selenite earthy marls containing frequently minute fragments of pumice, selenite, strata of volcanic ashes, seams of bitumen, and springs of petroleum (Barbadoes tar). Coralline rocks occupy six-sevenths of the whole area, rise in terraces to the height of above 100 feet, and are occasionally precipitous as a wall.

Scotland District contains various modifications of tertiary rocks, but with an original uniformity. The stratification is sometimes wavy, at other times greatly contorted, the earthy marl—indurated argillæ—or, as the colonists call it, chalk, occurs in masses from a few inches in thickness to a depth of several hundred feet. The summit of Mount Hillaby consists of this substance. Thin seams of bituminous coal and wood have been observed. A hill near Consets Bay is said to have been set on fire by a slave and to have burnt for *five years*. The marks of fire which the clays on the slope and at the foot of the hill still show, confirm the popular tradition.

There is a cavern in the parish of St. Lucy's, much visited by travellers on account of a remarkable species of zoophyte found there, which has gained it the name of the animal flower cave. In an excavation or basin filled with sea water, there is an oblong rock clothed with variegated sea moss, from among which issue small stems or tubes, from whose summit petals like those of the single marigold suddenly expand; but as soon as the hand approaches to pluck the seeming flower, the petal-like organs retract, and the stem disappears in the crevice whence it issued.

The most awful hurricane on record which has occurred in Barbadoes took place in 1780. Admiral Rodney stated that "the heavy cannon were carried upwards of 100 feet from the forts, and Governor Cunninghame assured the Secretary of State that a 12-pounder had been carried by the winds and waves from the south to the north battery, a distance of 140 yards. The loss of life was estimated at 4326 souls ; that of property at 1,320,564£ sterling. Not a single house or building, how-ever strong or sheltered, escaped uninjured ; most of the live stock and horned cattle perished ; the canes, corn, and ground provisions were utterly destroyed."

" In August, 1831, another hurricane occurred, in which 1591 persons, and property to the value of 1,602,800£., were destroyed. A sum of 100,000£. was voted by Parliament for the relief of the sufferers in Barbadoes, St. Vincent, and St. Lucia, of which the first-named island received one-half."—Martin's *British Colonies*, pp. 111—121.

___

" The negroes here differ much, I think, from those in the other islands, not only in manner, but even in form and physi-ognomy ; they are of a heavier build, broader in the face and higher in the forehead.   They are also certainly less good humoured, and more inclined to insolence ; so that if anything be gained in intelligence, it is lost in conduct.   On the whole, I do not think that the Barbadoes negroes are more intelligent than others I have met.   It is probable that this may come from more continual occupation."—Trollope's *West Indies*, p. 207.

Mr. Trollope's estimate of the Barbadian negro differs widely from my own.   He would, of course, have had the best opportu-nities of forming an opinion, as he resided on shore, whereas I generally slept on board the ship.   My own conclusion is arrived at on comparing them with the blacks of Brazil, Cuba, and the remainder of the West Indian Islands, which are the only countries I have visited where the negro forms a prominent feature of the population.—[ED.]

CHAPTER II.

ST. VINCENT AND ST. LUCIA.

THE *St. George* anchored in Kingston Bay, St. Vincent, at eight, a.m., on the 2nd March, 1861. Several merchantmen were lying in the harbour on our arrival, profusely decorated with flags and ever-greens in honour of the Prince's visit. His Royal Highness, with Major Cowell and Captain Egerton, landed almost immediately, and were received at the landing-place by what was intended to be a twenty-one gun salute; but which was rather a failure, in consequence of their being unable to get the guns to explode faster than about one in every two minutes, so that by the time they arrived at the end of the salute, the procession was well out of sight. However, it wont do to growl at their having made the most of limited means.

We were informed that as many officers as liked might join the procession, but that two only of each mess could be accommodated at the *déjeuner*. On reaching Government House, however, which is situated some distance beyond the town, all who

had gone ashore had their inner man looked after
in the most satisfactory manner. After lunch was
over, three of my brother officers were offered seats
in the carriage of a gentleman who was about to
return to the town. He was a very convivial party
indeed, and had not failed to do ample justice in
champagne to the toasts, "loyal and patriotic,"
which the worthy Governor had proposed ; a proceeding which had resultéd in his having become,
albeit very jolly, exceedingly obstinate. This failing
led him, in spite of G——'s remonstrances, to trials
of speed with every trap he overtook ; the ultimate
result being, that the horse, unable to stop himself,
ran *chest on* into a gun placed in the street as a
pillar of protection to foot-passengers against
vehicles, which not only spoilt the horse, but
caused those behind him to pick themselvés up in
the gutter, with the chaise enveloping them like a
conch-shell, one of the officers being seated on the
cocked hat of the other. Strange to say, no one
was hurt, a torn epaulette being the only damage
done. Truly, a special angel watches over naval
officers and—no, I wont couple "drunken men"
with "naval officers," but soften it down and say—
inebriated individuals.

The driver seemed rather pleased than otherwise,
merely remarking, that it wasn't the first time !

Another guest was rash enough to trust a friend
to take home his wife with her nurse and baby, as

he was unable at the time to accompany them himself. On following them shortly afterwards, he beheld to his dismay, on coming to a turn in the road, the carriage smashed to pieces, and its precious freight all of a heap together, the horse having disappeared. On finding they were all right, however, he took the matter in the most philosophical manner imaginable, seeming to regard it merely as an ordinary " incident of travel." If the amount of champagne consumed was any index of Vincelonian loyalty, they certainly are largely gifted in that way.

It being Saturday night, the ball, which had been originally intended to commence at nine and end at two, a.m., was arranged to commence at seven and end at twelve, so as not to infringe on the hours of Sunday. About eighteen of us (myself among the number) went. It took place in a large-sized room, fairly got up in the way of decoration. A somewhat meagre band of brass instruments formed the orchestra. The stewards were particularly attentive in introducing us to partners. About two-thirds of the guests present were white, and the presence of the remaining third, which consisted of the coloured individuals in the room, seemed to distress them much. By the word *coloured*, I mean any of those thousand-and-one tints varying from pale sepia and slightly *wavy* hair, to coal-black and unmistakeable *wool*. I find that the governing powers are frequently placed on the horns of awkward dilemmas by the negro element in colonial society. The coloured ones say, and with good reason too, it must be confessed, "We have subscribed to this fête" (or whatever it may be) "as well as you. Some of us are as well educated as any whites on the island. Our fathers, like yours, were many of them planters. Why, then, exclude us? Are we not 'men and brethren'? We wont stand it; and if you treat us in such a scurvy manner, beware." And so as these same coloured individuals are in many cases members of colonial councils, or at all events possess political votes, the unhappy governor of a West Indian island is obliged to be civil to them, and of course finds that he only escapes the black frying-pan to fall into the white fire.

Talking of *colour* prejudices, I remember an amusing little scene alongside the ship while we were lying here. A boat manned by four sturdy negroes, and steered by one who, although well dressed, appeared at a slight distance as black as the blackest of them, approached the gangway while one of our boats was coming alongside. In spite of our sentry's hails, and apparently also the remonstrances of the " coloured gentleman" in the stern, the boat's crew would keep pulling. At length, provoked by their stupidity, one of our officers vociferated, "Keep out of the way, you infernal niggers, in that boat there;"—a hail which met with a prompt reply from the individual in the stern, who shouted out, " Yes, sah ; you quite right, sah ; dey's all a parsall of infernal niggas, dey got no sense whatebber:" a decided case of the pot calling the kettle black. But to return to my description of the ball.

After finishing one of the dances, I was about to hand my partner to a seat beside which a chair was occupied by a woolly-headed young lady. I was considerably astonished to see her start back as if she had trodden on a snake, draw her clothes round her, and immediately leave that portion of the room; she at the same time exclaiming, in a low voice, " Not here, please—ugh !" (shiver.) The lady, too, was one whom I should not have suspected of possessing such a strong prejudice against her coloured sisters.

I read an entertaining article some time ago on the subject of " Colour-blindness." What a blessing it would be to the darkies if this disease only existed in the West Indies, and the whites couldn't tell the difference between an Indian-ink tint and a pale flesh colour !

It was originally intended that we should leave the harbour for St. Lucia on Sunday night; but arrangements having been made for the Prince and a party to visit the Souffrière (a volcano at the other end of the island), our route was altered, and at four, a.m., on Monday morning we weighed and steamed down the coast till we arrived off the foot of the mountain, which was about nine, a.m.

Several persons belonging to the island came round in us. Amongst others was a gentleman who was supposed to be the guest of one of our messmates, who, however, rebutted the charge in the most vigorous manner. But there he was on board, so, as in duty bound, we did our best as hosts towards him. He was weak-minded enough to indulge in a glass or two of ship's rum, and seemed to be much astonished at the difficulty he experienced in keeping his legs in a perpendicular position when he rose from the table. By some means he found his way into the starboard dickey on the poop, and finding therein the surgeon of the ship, essayed to enter into conversation with him. He assured him that "the moshun of th' ship affected a lanshman ver' mush," and was proceeding to make further remarks on the peculiar feelings experienced on board by "lanshmen," when——!

The after-guard had a nice job in the morning, and so had the side-cleaners. Champagne, rum, and sardines combined had done their work most effectually. It is a subject of speculation to the present day where he slept.

About twenty-four of us in all went ashore. Nearly every one got a mule or horse ; but I being, like the little boat, "a long way behind," could not raise so much as a donkey. However, I had come

to see the Souffrière, and see it I would ; so I persuaded a small nigger to act as guide, and started
on foot. The heat was intense ; and though I put
a white handkerchief over my cap, nothing but
great self-delusion could persuade me that I had on
a cool head-dress. The volcano is, I believe, over
3000 feet in height ; and by the time I had reached
an altitude of 1000 feet, I was regularly winded,
and began to think it would have been much
wiser to have remained at the bottom. However,
having started, I did not like to turn back, so I
toiled on, resting every now and then, to the unconcealed contempt of the little black boy, who, I
firmly believe, would have ascended Chimborazo
itself without stopping or feeling the slightest inconvenience. After the most fatiguing tramp I
ever had in my life, I reached the first ridge—oh,
what a pleasure it was to once more walk on a level
pathway ! Just then H—— overtook me on a mule
which he, more fortunate than me, had procured from
some good-natured planter. He gave me a drink
from his flask, which somewhat revived me ; and I
shouted with delight at overtaking, a few yards
further on, the canteen-man, who had charge of the
bottled beer. H—— and I immediately tackled a
bottle, drinking its contents from the neck ; and I
am quite sure that we never in our lives before knew
the delights of a bottle of Bass's pale ale. How we
revelled in that draught ! How we blessed the

thoughtful provider of it! I am perfectly convinced that had I not at that precise moment
overtaken that man, I should have given in, and
been picked up in a state of syncope on the return
of the party from the crater.

" It is a long lane," they say, " which has no
turning ;" and I began to think that the lane I
was traversing was a very long one indeed ; but,
true to the spirit of the proverb, it came to an
end at last ; and the welcome sight of the rest of
our party dispelled my feeling of fatigue, and informed me that I had walked up a mountain over
3000 feet in height.

The Souffrière has two craters, the old and the
new. The former consists of a circular basin,
about two miles in circumference. At a depth
of about 800 feet from the edge lies a small lake,
which consists of fresh, drinkable water. The
sides of the crater are clothed with foliage, which
sets off the water, giving it the appearance of a
clear mirror in an emerald-green frame ; there is
nothing about the appearance of the place to indicate that it is the crater of a not yet extinct volcano. The last eruption took place, from the new
crater, in 1813. It is now quiescent, no smoke
being visible ; but it is said that sulphureous and
bituminous fumes are frequently perceptible. I
was unable to find any pure lava ; but scoria and
tufa were abundant. A great quantity of fused

granite was lying about, and light ash seemed to be the prevailing material on the sides of the crater.*

Sir F. Thesiger, now Lord Chelmsford, when very young, resided here; and left the island, it is said, in consequence of his estate being destroyed in the eruption of 1813.

When I reached the remainder of our party, I found a capital lunch spread out on the grass. A glass of porter was exceedingly refreshing after my long walk, and I did not forget to do justice to the eatables; in fact, everybody's appetite seemed sharpened by the air and exercise. I know that *I* had a pretty good allowance of the latter, what-ever any one else may have had. Catch me walking up 3000 feet again!

There is a ridge between the old and new craters which it is not considered safe to cross. Two of my messmates, however, did so, and re-turned in safety.

One of the gentlemen present having kindly offered me his mule to make the descent, I mounted and followed the others. And now began a series of the most extraordinary gymnastic exercises I ever had to undertake. One minute I found myself embracing the neck of the animal I rode in the most affectionate manner; and I'm sure I pulled hair enough out of his mane to make thirty fiddle-bows. And when the beast's fore legs were lowest, and I

* See Notes, p. 33.

had to sit back till I got right on to his tail, he
evinced his dislike to my seat on that part of his
body by turning round—a dangerous proceeding
occasionally, where a false step would have capsized
the two of us down a declivity of about 150 feet.
One of our officers *did* go over, but, fortunately for
himself, parted company from his horse before
reaching the bottom, where the shrubs and vegetation broke his fall.

. I much regretted that I could not stop to gather
some magnificent tropical ferns, which were growing
in abundance on the mountain-side. W—— killed,
or had given to him, two snakes, each about four
and a half feet in length. The way he stuffed them
into his pocket—exclaiming, " I hope the beggars
are dead !"—was highly amusing. For my own
part, I should prefer a different sort of reptile cage;
but tastes differ. There are but three kinds of
snakes in St. Vincent, and they are all harmless.

There was some little surf on when we embarked,
so that we had to get niggers to carry us out to the
boat; not pick-a-back but baby fashion.

We left at half-past six, p.m., on the 4th March,
for St. Lucia, where we arrived on the morning of
the 5th, at half-past ten, a.m.

Castries Bay, in which we anchored, is one of the
prettiest harbours I ever saw. I much regret that
I am unable to give an idea of this place with the
pencil; but somehow or other, the bump of design,

or whatever it may be called, was denied me by nature, or perhaps, according to phrenological theory, is *counteracted* by another bump — say, that of disarrangement, for instance, a quality which my friends assure me I possess a large share of.

It has just struck me that I shall be getting into a scrape with critics if I don't abandon the habit I have of using the nominative personal pronoun ; but really I (there's the confounded letter again!) don't see how it is to be avoided. Could not some one give us an article, in one of the current magazines, entitled " I's and no I's," with illustrations?

But to return to St. Lucia. On our arrival a general invitation was given to the officers of the ship to attend the ball to be given in the evening in honour of the Prince. Sixteen gold-laced coats were present, and although the ball-room was small and the supper meagre, we did pretty well. On taking my partner down to supper, I found, to my horror, that I had made a mistake in coming down so soon, the Prince and the head swells of the island being only intended to occupy the room that time, as it would only hold about twenty people. However, I could not very well go back ; so seating the lady at the table, provided her with supper, and after that, proceeded to fortify my own inner man against the effects of the cold night air, by the aid of ham, chicken, and champagne. We got on board again about three o'clock.

St. Lucia contained, according to the census in 1851, 24,000 inhabitants, of which about 13,000 could speak English. Talking of inhabitants, I heard here, for the first time, a Yankee's idea of the meaning of that word, illustrated by the statement that a certain island, under Confederate dominion, "contained three inhabitants and twenty-seven niggers!"

There are three kinds of snakes in St. Lucia, the trigonocephalus, the crebo, and another, with the name of which I am unacquainted. The former is called on the island the "rat-tail," or "serpent jaure." A very good specimen was given to me, preserved in spirits. In Somerville's "Physical Geography" it is stated that "the yellow viper of the French West Indian Islands, the Trigono-cephalus lanceolatus, is one of the most dangerous snakes in existence."

I have heard that it is estimated that over a dozen people are yearly bitten and killed by this reptile. Martin's "British Colonies"—a most valuable work to any one visiting the West Indies—states nineteen as the average number of deaths per annum. The trigonocephalus subsists chiefly on rats, and abounds in sugar plantations.

It will hardly be credited that this, the most poisonous serpent which the world produces, frequently comes by his death by being *swallowed whole* by another snake no bigger than himself, and perfectly innocuous! yet such is the fact. When the crebo meets the rat-tail, " war to the knife " is the result, and the venomous snake can seldom escape the jaws of his hungry antagonist. A pair of these snakes, captured in this interesting position, *i.e.*, the rat-tail halfway down the crebo's throat, were brought on board for the Prince's acceptance, but were declined by him on the plea that it would be depriving the museum of the island of a valuable specimen were he to receive them.

The trigonocephalus is closely allied to the rattle-snake. It is sometimes called the "lance-headed snake of Martinique."

I found that the same feeling with regard to the coloured population prevailed at St. Lucia as at the other islands. It is needless to again enlarge on this subject of black *versus* white. I can only say that truly our West Indian colonists view the question in its *blackest* aspect.

NOTES ON CHAPTER II.

" In 1812 a tremendous eruption of La Souffrière took place, in which some lives and much property were lost. At noon on the 27th April, thirty days after the destruction of the Carracas, a severe concussion of the earth took place, and a black column of smoke burst from the crater, followed by volumes of *favilla*

D

(ash-coloured dust), which continued pouring forth for three days. On the evening of the 30th, the flames burst forth ; the rolling of the thunder became almost deafening ; sand and stones were ejected ; earthquakes were felt ; streams of lava poured down on either side ; the neighbouring estates were covered with scoriæ ; the channels of two rivers were blocked up, and some negroes killed. . . . . The eruption terminated on the 1st of May. The aspect of the mountain was greatly changed, the vegetation having been totally destroyed, the height diminished, old ravines closed up, a new crater formed near the old one, and both filled to a considerable depth with yellow-coloured water. . . . . The island of Barbadoes, fully sixty miles from St. Vincent, was shrouded for four hours in nearly total darkness, and the surface covered to the depth of several inches with the favillæ discharged from the crater, which proved a fertilizing agent of great power. . . . . The noise of the eruption, heard at Barbadoes and several other islands, was mistaken for the engagement of hostile fleets, and the troops were placed under arms."—Martin's *West Indies*, p. 128.

A very capital description of St. Lucia is contained in page 123 of the same work ; and in the next, a description of the celebrated Diamond Rock, which was fortified by Sir Samuel Hood in 1803.

"This memorable crag of grey limestone, 'shaped like a nine-pin, with the point a little broken at the summit,' was put upon the establishment of a sloop of war, with a complement of 150 men and boys, supplied with ammunition, stores, and provisions from Antigua or Barbadoes for six months. A thirty-two pounder was hoisted about half way up the rock, 360 feet above the water line, and the summit and other parts being also defended with guns, this natural fortress proved of great service to the squadron. . . . . This nondescript man-of-war did good service for two years and a-half, the height of its guns enabling it to effectually command the passage between it and Martinique, so that it was almost impossible for a vessel to enter Fort Royal." The French bombarded it in vain, for the solid rock resisted all shot, so at length they turned the attack into a blockade, and Captain Maurice and his brave band had to surrender, ' which they did on very honourable terms, losing three killed and wounded, while the enemy lost fifty.'

" St. Lucia is particularly · celebrated for its snakes. One cannot walk ten yards off the road—so one is told—without being bitten ; and if one is bitten, death is certain—except by the interposition of a single individual of the island, who will cure the sufferer for a consideration. Such at least is the report made on this matter. The first question one should ask on going there is the whereabouts and usual terms of that worthy and useful practitioner."—Trollope's *West Indies and Spanish Main*, p. 163.

CHAPTER III.

WE anchored on the 7th March, 1861, in the bay
of Fort Royal, Martinique.   On the right hand side
of the harbour is situated the fort which, I presume,
gives its name to the town, and which in 1794 was
the scene of one of those " deeds of naval daring"
which rendered the English name at that time so
famous throughout the Western Indies.   At the
attack on Martinique, Captain Faulkner, commanding his Majesty's brig *Zebra*, after standing a heavy
fire of grape from the fort for a considerable time,
to which his puny broadside could offer no effectual
return, suddenly ran the brig alongside, and in the
most gallant manner captured it by boarding from
the main-yard-arm.   As I looked on this scene of
bygone British prowess, I thought of Captain Marryat's " Peter Simple," and how the quartermaster
informed him that the fort was taken by a *coup-de-
main;* how the said Peter, being young and tender-

hearted, was bewitched by the charms of the beautiful Celeste. This, too, was the scene of the hurricane,
when—"I say, old chap, are there any bananas alongside?" recalled me back to the rude realities of the
present. I gave my messmate a reproachful look
(which didn't seem to affect him in the least), and
began to think of taking care of my stomach, for it
was tea-time.

After tea we went ashore to see the illuminations,
for the French were not a whit behind the English
colonists in giving a "warm reception" to Prince
Alfred; one, too, infinitely preferable to that which
is usually understood by that term. Very nicely
got up were the said illuminations. Our French
neighbours seem to have a talent for exhibitions of
that kind, which we more dull Saxons don't possess.

In the Savannah (as a large green square, surrounded by trees and situated near the landing-
place, is called) a number of black women were
performing what they called a native dance. Each
one carried a large silk flag, on which was written
in gilt letters an English or French inscription,
such as "God save the Queen," "Welcome, Prince
Alfred," "Vive l'Empereur," &c. &c. They were
dressed in the very highest style of nigger costume,
which consists of as many different colours as a
dress will admit of, and as many ornaments as the
body will bear without fatigue. Their wild yells

(for it was not singing), the demoniacal way in which they rushed about in the circle formed by the torch-bearers, the appearance of the black audience by which they were surrounded, grinning and shouting with excitement and delight; the square itself glittering with myriads of coloured lights, formed altogether one of the most picturesque (or more strictly speaking, perhaps, grotesque) sights imaginable. Two old men, seated on the grass, beat time on a couple of very primitive-looking tamborines. The noise was frightful, and had I chanced to come upon the scene unawares, I should have pronounced it to be possibly an Indian orgie; not by any means a performance got up by domesticated niggers.

There are queer stories told of the remnants of old Carib superstitions still lurking amongst the "dark ones" of these islands. In Barbadoes, and some others, there are no descendants from the aboriginal inhabitants now living, but the fugitive blacks who sought refuge in Martinique intermarried with the Caribs whom they found in possession, and therefore possess many distinctive peculiarities from the negroes of the other islands. I have also heard stories of rites celebrated, in which the African fetish played a large part, something being selected as fetish, and regarded with the reverence due to the name accordingly. This latter superstition was of course confined to bodies of blacks who had recently left Africa. Since the manumission of the slaves this sort of thing has ceased almost entirely.

After leaving the square we entered an hotel, in which a number of French officers were seated, smoking " long toms," and indulging in " vin ordinaire," at two francs the bottle. On seeing us they rose up, received us very politely, and in a few minutes we were fraternizing in the most satisfactory manner. They were determined to act as hosts, so we resigned ourselves to circumstances, finding it was no use to remonstrate against having our glasses repeatedly filled with champagne and " rom ponsh," which latter is a Frenchman's idea of a thoroughly national English beverage. After finishing a moderate-sized soup tureen full of the said " ponsh," we adjourned in company to the rooms of a student at the hospital, whose devotion to the cause of science was manifested by the presence of a tall skeleton, which the owner seemed to regard with a sort of parental affection. We were assured that he had been a " gens-d'armes" in Paris. Why a *soldier's* skeleton should be of more value than a civilian's I'm sure I can't say, but it struck me as an illustration of our Gallic neighbours' fondness for military affairs. We returned on board about ten, p.m.

Now the 8th March happened, this year of 1861, to be one of the forty which all good Catholics are bound to observe as days of self-denial and reflection; in plain English, it was Lent; and therefore when the Governor of the island proposed to give a ball, in compliment to a member of the royal family of *perfide Albion*, the bishop, or ecclesiastical functionary commanding for the time being, put his veto on it, by observing that sacrament should not be given to any ladies who so far forgot the season of the year as to be guilty of dancing. However, the governor gave his ball, and about forty ladies braved ecclesiastical displeasure and came, though I am afraid they had to pay for it afterwards, as one remarked to me (in French, of course) in the most ingenuous manner, " that there would be the devil to pay to-morrow," or words to that effect. As there were three times as many gentlemen present as ladies, I found great difficulty in getting a partner, so after two or three dances I gave up entirely, and devoted myself to cigars and weak lemonade in the court-yard. After a time some one proposed to go and look for the supper-room ; so we searched about, ashamed to ask for directions, at one time finding ourselves in the kitchen, and a few minutes afterwards in the guard-room, but no supper-table could we find. At length the conviction reached our minds that *there was no supper*. Can you imagine the feelings of a British, naval officer when he learns that he has been asked to a ball with no feed

at the end? I draw a veil over our feelings. Some
sorrows cannot find expression in words.

Do not, my dear reader, run away with the idea
that we are a greedy set of individuals because we
wanted supper. Far from it. I don't suppose that
any of us would have eaten enough to be called a
light lunch, but the familiar scramble was wanting,
and with "Nix mangiare" ringing in our ears, we
smoked our cigars in mournful silence.

Our boat had been ordered at half-past one, a.m.,
but the dancing finished earlier than we had anticipated; at half-past twelve they put out the lights,
on which unmistakeable hint to go we were obliged
to leave the shelter of the house and walk down to
the landing-place in the drizzling rain which had
begun to fall, and wetted us through. Finding that
our boat had not arrived, the Frenchmen good-
naturedly offered us a passage off in theirs, which
offer our commander accepted.

On Saturday morning, the 9th March, we weighed
and ran down to "St. Pierre," the commercial capital of the island. As viewed from the anchorage, it
is decidedly the prettiest port we have visited.
Some of us went ashore in the evening, and found
our way to the "Hotel des Bains," to meet by ap-
pointment some of our naval friends in the *Bellone*
(which vessel, I think, I omitted to state is a screw-
frigate of thirty-six guns). After waiting there a

short time, we proceeded arm-in-arm to the " Jardins
Botaniques," where there were to be grand doings
in the way of illuminations and fireworks.   It is
astonishing what a universal tendency naval officers
of all nations have to behave in the same manner
when ashore.   We (for I could not help myself, being
taken possession of by M. T——, the stout assistant-
surgeon) formed in line abreast right across the
street, parting only for ladies.   Anybody else had
to get by the best way he could.   " A man is known
by the company he keeps."   Had we met our own
or any other captain at this precise moment, the
company I was in I am afraid would not have reflected much credit on me, as they were singing
songs, comic, sentimental, and political; the
latter I fear not of the most orthodox tendency.

We arrived at the gardens too late for the fireworks; but the illuminations (which were still to
be seen) were splendid.   Thousands of Chinese
lanterns were hanging from the branches of the
magnificent palms and other tropical trees with
which the gardens abounded.   Illuminated arches
spanned the paths, and the banks of the pretty
little lake in the centre of the grounds were brilliantly lit up, the many-coloured lights being reflected back from its calm surface till it appeared
one blaze of light.   The splendour of the scene
realized one's ideas of an Oriental festival.   Even

in China, "the land of lanterns," I never saw anything so pretty.

A *serpent jaune* (one of those deadly snakes previously mentioned, and which is a native of Martinique as well as of St. Lucia) had been found
coiled round one of the trees by one of the men
employed in lighting the lamps, and having been
immediately killed, lay dead at its foot; the head
lancet-shaped, flat, and very broad, needed but a
casual glance from any one who has lived in places
where snakes abound, to be pronounced that of a
most deadly species.

After going round the gardens, we returned as
we came. On reaching the hotel, some others of
our messmates joined us, and we proceeded to fulfil
those national duties of drinking first of all to each
other's healths, and then to those of our respective
sovereigns. Then the fun grew "fast and furious,"
and our allies showed that they were capable of
making as much noise upon occasion as any equal
number of Englishmen. At length a glass acci-
dentally dropped by one of our party cut open the
forehead of one of the *aspirants*, a piece of it having
ricocheted from the marble table. It was a pretty
deep cut, though he made light of it; the surgeon
present bandaged it up, however, and this checked
the noise. We soon after left the hotel; and they
finding that it was utterly impossible for us to procure a boat on the beach, again, as on a former

occasion, offered us theirs, and, in fact, insisted on taking us off; and so ended our evening.

On the morning of Sunday, the 10th March, we left Martinique, and at three, p.m., anchored in Roseau roads, Dominica.*

On Monday several of us went ashore. The party visited the sulphur springs, and described them on their return as a large cavern from which steam and occasionally water is ejected. The ebullition of the water sounded "like the boiling of a hundred kettles." The water was hot enough to scald the hand if immersed in it. At Dominica there exists a precipice, of about 250 feet in depth, to which is attached the following story. "I tell the tale as it was told to me;" and though I cannot vouch for the accuracy of the details, the main facts are undoubtedly correct. I believe they took place some twenty years ago.

Captain M——, the hero of the story, was returning on horseback from a picnic with a party of friends on the summit of the mountain. Having drunk a few glasses of the champagne, &c., which always flows freely on such occasions, he was, although sober, rather reckless. The rest of his party were some little distance behind him—at all events, out of sight—and after riding on for a short way, he came to a sort of low rocky wall which he

* So called from having been discovered by Columbus on Sunday, November 3rd, 1493.

tried to make his horse jump. The animal for a
long time refused the leap, nor could any amount
of coaxing or horsemanship induce him to take
what, under ordinary circumstances, his rider would
have considered a mere nothing.

At length, having given him a good run, he dug
his spurs into the horse and got him over; but his
horror may be imagined, when instead of, as he
expected, level ground, *a sheer pitch of* 250 *feet* was
the unwelcome spectacle to the terrified horseman.
No earthly power apparently could save him, and
he has since said that in the awful moment occupied by his descent, he seemed to have time enough
to recollect every action of his life—a power of the
mind which I have frequently heard of as being
developed under similar circumstances. When they
reached the bottom, the horse was killed instanta-
neously, but the rider, strange to say, *only had his
ankles broken*. His friends, who had safely reached
home without him, became alarmed at his absence,
and next day sent out a party in search of him.
They retraced the road, and at length came to the
spot where the horse had refused to jump, a fact
which was evident from the positions of the hoof
marks; but they never for a moment imagined he
had gone over the precipice. At length, after
much fruitless searching, some one happened to
look over the rock, and beheld, to his surprise, his
unfortunate friend and what remained of his horse,

at the bottom. They descended and found him
lying insensible. A hasty litter was constructed,
and he was carried home. Placed under proper
medical care, he recovered, and was in six months'
time as well as ever. At the present moment he
is, I believe, Colonel of a line regiment in England.
The place still goes by the name of Captain
M——'s Leap.

The usual processions, &c., took place in the forenoon, on the Prince's landing, and a ball (which we
cared a great deal more about) in the evening.
The ball-room was a sort of bare deal barn, generally used, I believe, as the Governor's drawing-
room. The company was of the most miscella-
neous description as far as colour went, embracing
all shades, from coal black to very freckled white.
" Variety is charming," saith the proverb; but
only a very small proportion of this variety was at
all charming in our opinion. What a bore this
colour question is again; but it *will* turn up whenever one writes, talks, or speaks of a West Indian
island, where one has not only to study the colour
of one's dress, but the colour also of one's acquaintances.

It is the greatest fun possible to see two darkies
trying a gallop or waltz. Every woolly-headed
young lady has as much action as a cavalry horse,
and jumps up and down in the most absurd manner; and as *step* seems to be an unknown accom-

plishment, their performance is generally highly
amusing. Notwithstanding this mixture of black
and white (which produced on the eye the effect of
a pepper-and-salt mixture when viewed from a
trifling elevation), we had very good fun—the
quantity and quality of the supper were both very
good, so that, at all events, we had something or
other to console ourselves with, if we did lack
partners. Our own band formed the orchestra.
The anchor was weighed immediately on our return on board, and at about half-past two, a.m., we
bid farewell to Dominica.

I have attempted no description of this island, as
the quotation in the foot-note conveys a far better
idea than my own words will supply of its general
appearance. They are from the clever pen of the
author of " Framley Parsonage."*

* " To my mind, Dominica, as seen from the sea, is by far the
most picturesque of all these islands. Indeed, it would be difficult to beat it either in colour or in grouping. It fills one
with an ardent desire to be off and rambling among those green
mountains—as if one could ramble through such wild bush
country, or ramble at all, with the thermometer at 85°. But
when one has only to think of such things, without any idea of
doing them, neither the bushes nor the thermometer are considered.

" One is landed at Dominica on a beach. If the water be
quiet, one gets out dry-shod by means of a strong jump ; if the
surf be high, one wades through it ; if it is very high, one is of
course upset. * * *

" And then the perils of the surf being passed, one walks into
the town of Roseau. It is impossible to conceive a more dis-

After about eight hours' run, the *St. George* cast anchor in Basseterre roads, Guadaloupe, and scarcely had she done so than we, *i.e.*, the junior officers, received a message from those of the *Bellone* requesting our company that evening to supper, which was to take place ashore at the house of one of the surgeons of the hospital. As might have been expected, the meeting was *not* the quietest I ever witnessed. There were eight from the French frigate, four army officers, three from the hospital, and eight of ourselves. The arrangements for the supper in the way of knives, forks, and glasses, were somewhat defective, but in other respects they were pretty good. Our carte included, amongst other things, some most dyspepsia-provoking pastry, which bore in its composition, I suspect, a great similarity to Australian Damper. Did you ever taste damper? No! Well, then you have an experience yet to undergo in the way of eating flour and water.

Our vivacious friends were as noisy as they had been on the previous occasions we were in their company.   M. T——, the stout party before

tressing sight. Every house is in a state of decadence. There are no shops that can properly be so called. The people wander about, idle, chattering, and listless ; the streets are covered with thick rank grass ; there is no sign either of money made or of money making. Everything seems to speak of desolation, apathy, and ruin. There is nothing even in Jamaica so sad to look at as the town of Rosean. Coffee is the chief export from Dominica."

referred to afforded us great amusement. He is not
a baby by any means, either in voice or corporation,
but fearing that he would not be heard plainly enough
unless raised above our level (he had lungs that
would have roared a bull down), he mounted a chair,
performed a species of double shuffle, during which
we fully expected him to have gone through the
cane bottom, and requested silence as he was about
to say a few words in English.

Silence being obtained, M. T—— looked round
in a benign manner and said, O yez! (Oh, yes.)

Of course every one laughed, and various parties
shouted out, " Go a-head, old fellow ;" " Drive on,"
and other encouraging sentences of similar import.

But M. T—— imagined that we were pressing
him to repeat his words, so he again said—O yez!

This was the extent of his English vocabulary.
As one involuntarily laughed whenever he said this,
so droll was his manner, he had come to the conclusion that it was something eminently funny.

And so the evening passed away as such evenings
generally do. Songs, toasts, and—very little senti-
ment—abounded. By way of winding up, we sang
both national airs at the same time, which produced
a delightful discord, and our friends marched down
to the boat singing in a way which I fully expected
would draw upon them the polite attentions of the
police. Many were the heads protruded from first
story windows, and vehement were the expostula-

tions addressed by their night-capped owners to
these midnight disturbers of their slumbers—ex-
postulations which, as might be imagined, didn't in
the slightest degree interfere with their proceedings.

Several parties came off to visit the ship the next
day, and amongst them a fair proportion of pretty
faces.

Two individuals dined on board in the evening, one
of whom was a most singular looking little party.
He was, I believe, a magistrate or something of the
sort, but—mind, it's only a suspicion—had had a
leetle drop too much of Moselle. I say *Moselle*, because
that was the last thing I saw him drinking.   Well,
this little gentleman, on coming on the main deck
to smoke, began to give us practical illustrations of
various dancing steps, which not only made us roar
with laughter, but induced the belief that at some
bygone period of his life he had been a dancing
master.   His leaps were only bounded by the beams
which supported the upper deck, and having once or
twice come in contact with them, he for a few moments became grave and thoughtful, from which he
only rallied on being offered a cigar. He then joined
in a quadrille, in which his movements were eccentric
in the extreme, finally subsiding from sheer fatigue.
He landed in the 9.40 boat, and M—— with some
one else accompanied him to his house to see him
safely disposed of; for since his Terpsichorean feats on

board, he had indulged in a glass of grog, which had somewhat impaired his balancing powers. It appears that they saw him safely to bed, and left him with a candle burning in his room; but that they no sooner departed than he jumped up, began singing and "kicking up a row" and tried to light a cigar. They returned, however, and put a stop to such proceedings. Three several times did this happen; so as a last resource they *tied him down in bed with his sheet* and came off.

I much regretted that I had no opportunity of visiting the still active volcano. G—— and M—— rodé part of the way up, and then dismounting, clambered up to the lower crater. They say that the smell of sulphur was overpowering. The smoke rendered the bottom partially invisible, and the rocks around were covered with a reddish sulphurous deposit. G—— brought on board some pieces of lava.

Of course during the time we were amusing ourselves as above described, Prince Alfred was undergoing the civilities of the authorities. I doubt, however, whether he enjoyed himself more than we did.

There are an immense number of Chinamen to be seen both at Guadaloupe and Martinique. These deluded individuals are, I believe, called free apprentices, which apparently means a person who gets all the kicks and none of the halfpence which

fall to the lot of a purchased slave. At least, such
was the definition of their position given to us by
our French naval friends.

I cannot help noticing the infinite superiority of
Basseterre (and Fort Royal, also, I may add) to
the ports in the English islands, in the way of
pierage accommodation. My journal contains
several remarks on this subject, but as Trollope
has noticed this in his flying sketch of these places,
entitled "Passage of the Windward Islands," I
will not further enlarge on here.

And now we must bid farewell to Guadaloupe. I
have a lingering reluctance to do so, so pleasant are
the memories of its clean trim streets and its civil
inhabitants.

The next island which the *St. George* visited was
Antigua—one whose name deserves to be handed
down to posterity with all honour, as being the
first to advocate of itself the abolition of negro
slavery. I can fancy I hear some indignant (theo-
retical) abolitionist, of the weaker sex, exclaiming,
"Well, and so they ought to have; they only did
their duty!" Not so fast, my dear madam; put
yourself in the same position. We will suppose
you had been left a legacy, to which in a legal
point of view you had an undoubted right, but
which, after you had arrived at years of discretion,
you learnt was the result of an enormous fraud
perpetrated on a family whose descendants were at

the present moment begging their bread. We will further suppose, that by giving up all claim to this money, you would be reduced from comparative wealth to a bare independence. Would it not require a strong effort of virtuous feeling to restore it to the rightful owners? Well, this was just the position of the Antigonians; and therefore I say, all honour to them for it. Recollect, ye red-hot abolitionists, that *British* ships and *British* capitalists established slavery, and do not wonder that the sins of the fathers still bear fruit (as witness America) in the misdeeds of the children. Do not mistake me. No one more than myself would vote for the total extinction of slavery; but, in my opinion, abolitionists of the present day are men, who, with the best of hearts, have the worst of heads, inasmuch as they advocate the immediate emancipation of hundreds of thousands of blacks who have neither the means, energy, or education to support themselves. No, no; gradual must be the process by which the debased and demoralized African can in a country like the States of America be trusted with the responsibilities of free citizenship.

But I am forgetting that the "Cruise of the *St. George*" has very little to do with negroes, bond or free; or, at all events, with any discussion of their rights or wrongs; so having eased my conscience by a little piece of high-flown declamation,

I will return whence I started—the anchorage of
St. John's Harbour, Antigua.

There is nothing particularly picturesque about
this island. Indeed, were it not for the temperature and the unenviable notoriety the place possesses for sharks, it might be any haven in
England, from Dover to Land's-end. There are
few of the distinctive features of tropical vegetation
to be seen at the distance we lay from the shore.

A procession, lunch (I beg their pardons, *déjeuner*), and presentation took place here, as
elsewhere; in fact, so universal was the loyalty
manifested throughout the West Indian colonies
to the son of our beloved Queen, and so similar
were the arrangements at each island, varied only
by the intelligence, money, and pieces of ordnance
at the disposal of their town councils, that a description of one serves for that of all.

Antigua ranks next in importance to Barbadoes,
being the seat of a bishopric. The only natural
curiosities I was able to obtain were stuffed
frogs, beetles, a peculiar description of white seaweed, and several varieties of petrified woods,
which, together with jasper, may be picked up in
large quantities.* Stuffed guanas were also to

---

* The geology of Antigua struck me as affording an interesting study to lovers of that science, so I shall again quote Mr.
Martin's valuable work :—

"Three distinct classifications of the tertiary formation have

be purchased; but as the process of preserving them had reduced their skins to a jet black colour washed over with a varnish, which though eminently well calculated to catch flies, precluded all idea of packing them in any material softer than iron shavings, I did not invest in one; especially as (putting aside the question of packing them) they presented only the appearance of a melancholy burlesque on the real animal.

The town of St. John, which is the capital of Antigua, is the most promising looking and well kept we have yet visited. Of course they gave us a ball, and, equally a matter of course, we went to it. But, stop; I shall be getting into trouble. They gave H.R.H. Prince Alfred a ball.—No, that

been noted. On a general view, the island consists of a rocky conglomerate of the newest fleotztrap, such as wacke, porphyry, trap, breccia, amygdaloid, and some spherical masses of basaltic greenstone. This occupies the hilly district in the south and west; the north and east divisions exhibit calcareous marl and coarse sandstone, interspersed with blocks of tolerably compact limestone; the interior exhibits argillaceous strata of varied character and extensive irregular beds of coarse chert or flint. No organic fossils, except immense sharks' teeth and marine exuviæ, have been discovered. Petrified woods, with the distinctive and delicate fibres of palms and dycotyledonous trees, perfectly preserved, are found associated with chert, or on the surface of the conglomerate and the marl with agate, cornelian, and chalcedony. Nitrate of silver sometimes covers like a hoarfrost the flat oozy shore on the north and east."—Martin's *British Colonies*, p. 145.

"Antigua was named by Columbus in honour of a church in Seville, *Santa Maria la Antigua*."—*Ibid*. p. 143.

wont do.   They gave a ball in honour of the
Prince's visit—that is the phrase—which we attended.   About 200 ladies were present, and,
mirabile dictu, not a single one whose hair re-
sembled the contents of a horsehair mattress.   I
expect they had to bear a good deal of abuse for it
afterwards.   I overheard an amusing dialogue at
the door.   A well-dressed black presented himself
for admittance.   (The ball, I should have stated,
took place in the upper story of the Court house,
and one or two negro soldiers formed the sentries
placed on the landing-place.)

"You can't pass heah.   I hab ordahs dat no
negro be admitted."

" Who the devil are you calling a negro, sir?
Don't you see, sir, I'm a gentleman?"

" Yes, sah, a coloured generalman.   It's all de
same, niggah or coloured generalman."

Here the " coloured gentleman " tried to push
into the doorway, and was immediately collared by
the sentry, who did not disguise his contempt for
the "gentleman."

"By golly, sah, you try dat, I kick you down
'tairs.   I tell you I got orders dat no coloured
person go into de ball-room."

" Silence, you infernal ——!"

" I tell you, you *is* a coloured person," shouted
the sentry, losing his temper ; " so you jest go out
of dis."

Here they came to struggling; the sentry trying to push the gentleman downstairs, and the latter delivering blows on the soldier's face and head, which might as well have been bestowed on a cocoa-nut, for all the attention he paid to them.

Suddenly one of the stewards appeared, and seeing the scrimmage, said, "Hallo, what is the matter here? What are you about, you black scoundrel, trying to push that gentleman downstairs? Let him up, sir, directly!"

" Why, sah, Mr. —— (the manager of the ball) give me ordahs dat no coloured pusson whatebber pass trough de door; and I's sure dis individual *is* a coloured pusson, dough he say he ain't."

The steward bit his lips to conceal a smile, said, " All right, my good man; I'll be answerable," and passed the stranger in.

This exemplifies a nigger's respect for his own colour. It is generally believed that he would take the ugliest white face ever placed on man's shoulders in exchange for his own. He does not believe in an *intellectual* black.

We left Antigua on the 18th March, 1861, at six, a.m., and arrived at Montserrat on the forenoon of the same day.

CHAPTER IV.

MONTSERRAT TO SANTA CRUZ.

At Montserrat, which was, I believe, so named by Columbus after a mountain of that name in Spain, we remained till five, a.m., on the 19th March. A riding party went ashore in company with the Prince. As I was not one of them, I can say nothing about the place beyond remarking that from the anchorage it appeared a very steep, mountainous island, in its general features like Dominica. There is a volcano here called, like most other West Indian ones, " La Souffrière;" and sulphur of inferior quality is obtained. It seems, from all accounts, to be a well-ordered, happy little island, and of course loyal to the backbone.

Between Montserrat and Nevis lies the island of Redonda. Every account of the West Indies mentions this queer-looking island. One likens it to a ship under sail, and another to a haycock, its appearance varying according to the point of view from which it is seen. For my own part, to tell the honest truth, I did not see it at all, so cannot indulge in any simile about it.*

Five hours' run from Montserrat brought us to the anchorage of Charlestown, the capital of Nevis, which is a small island to the southward of St. Kitts, from the coast of which it is visible. Nevis is a volcanic island, 3500 feet in height, and is chiefly interesting to naval men, from the fact of the old register in the church containing the record of Nelson's marriage (he was then Captain Horatio Nelson) with Mrs. Nesbit Willoughby. It was suggested by some well-meaning individual that a sight of this record would be particularly interesting to the Prince, and he felt rather damped by ——'s remark, that " the less said about *that* marriage the better."

Several of us landed for the purpose of riding. I got a capital little pony for the afternoon, for which I was only charged two shillings, and he proved amply worth his hire. The inhabitants were evidently unaccustomed to displays of naval horsemanship. We rode about ten miles, coming the greater part of the way back at a hand gallop; and as we passed groups of negroes on the road, we were assailed by their remonstrances : " Oh, massa, you ride dat hoss too fast altogedder," and other similar remarks, some of them by no means com-

---

· * Mr. Gosse, the naturalist, likens it to the well known Bass Rock.—Gosse's *Naturalist in Jamaica.*

plimentary, were addressed to each of us in turn by
the indignant darkies. ·

A ball, to which several of the officers went, concluded the day. Those who were there said it was
a very pleasant one. As I was not, the reader need
not be afraid of my again inflicting on him an
account of the numbers of white and black beauties
present, or a disquisition on the wrongs of our
" black bred'ren."

We left Nevis at ten minutes to ten, a.m., of the
20th March, and at twenty-five minutes to twelve
anchored in Basseterre Roads, St. Christopher, commonly called St. Kitts.

And now, my dear reader, prepare yourself for
another description of a landing and a ball. It is
not my fault that I have to record so many affairs
of this nature. Having undertaken to give an
account of our experiences, I could no more omit
the balls, than write an account of the Russian war
without the battles. Moreover, is not the ball the
" pièce de résistance" of the programme? They are
very dull to read about, I know; but, oh! they're
" so jolly" to go to. If, therefore, any one objects
to reading what I have to say about *this* ball, let
him turn over a few pages, and he shall be safely
landed on one of the demi-semi-populated islands
of the Virgin group, yclept Tortola.

And the black question?—anything about that?

No, nothing. I pledge my word of honour I will
avoid the creatures altogether. So now for the
landing-place.

A capital temporary pier had been erected by the
inhabitants for the accommodation of the Prince.
It so happened that several of us went ashore before
His Royal Highness left the ship, and, I am afraid,
caused considerable perturbation in the breasts of
the worthy town-council men, they being under the
impression that the Prince was coming sooner than
he ought to, and that as everything was not ready
for his reception, the infuriated townsfolk would
pitch into them as the responsible parties. On
landing, however, this delusion on their part was
dispelled, as the other officers who landed with me
were respectively two lieutenants and an officer of
the Royal Marines; and I myself, the youngest of
the party, being gifted by nature with hair which
impertinent people call carroty, but which I mildly
designate as *red*, did not present the regal aspect
which they naturally expected to find in a scion of
the Royal House of England. " *Him* de Prince;
de Prince not got hair like dat," was the *sotto voce*
remark I overheard from an elderly mulatto woman.

However, it is something, I suppose, to be mistaken for a prince even at a distance of thirty yards.

There exists only one hotel in the place, but that
is a very fair one.   On reaching it, I found an old

acquaintance, F—— of the B——,* who introduced
me to Mr. H——, the editor of a local paper.
Mr. H—— kindly offered to drive us to see a sugar-
mill, an offer which we were delighted to accept;
so, mounting his trap (which had evidently never
made the acquaintance of Longacre), away we went.
After a three · miles' drive, we reached the estate of
Mr. Branch, who, in the most polite manner, showed
us all over the mill (a steam one), and explained to
us the whole art and mystery of making sugar.
By the bye, sugar is made in a much more cleanly
manner than I had imagined; and the belief I had
hitherto entertained in the possibility of breeches-
buttons, or locks of wool, being found to be the
nucleus of those crystallized lumps which occasionally
figure in the domestic sugar-basin, was destroyed.
Observing, however, that there was nothing to prevent adventurous little nigger boys from climbing
to the tops of the molasses-hogsheads to immerse
and then suck their paws, I shall still cherish a
lurking belief that the story of the high-flavoured
treacle sold by the grocer of Deptford *may* be founded
on fact, as the planks are very slippery, and little
boys in all countries will be careless.

After seeing the mill, we returned to the town,
dined with Mr. H——, and then went to have a

* Poor F—— died at Port Royal, of yellow fever, in August
or September, 1861. He sleeps in that saddest of all burial-
places, the "Palisades." *Requiescat in pace.*

look at the ball-room. It was capitally decorated; and amongst the vegetable ornaments, the palm cabbage was one which was freely used. This cabbage (why so called I cannot imagine, as it resembles a horse's tail much more than a cabbage) is a long affair about three feet in length, enclosed in a covering not unlike in shape to a common rolling-pin, being thick in the centre, and tapering towards the ends. When denuded of this sheath, it resembles a military plume. I forgot to mention that when Prince Alfred was entertained by the Governor of Martinique, a gigantic cabbage tree, said to be 150 years old, and considered one of the curiosities of the island, was cut down to afford a dish: (each tree only produces one cabbage, and must be sacrificed to get at it):—an expensive way of showing politeness.

And now I come to that troublesome subject, the ball itself. F—— and myself drove to the door with Mr. H——. A body of volunteers lined the entrance, and from what I heard, had apparently been lining it ever since sunset. Oh, how tired those poor fellows looked! We were afraid we should have been late, but were an hour too early. Our band, which was to form the orchestra for the first half of the dances, had not yet made its appearance; and His Royal Highness and suite seemed in no hurry to make *theirs*.

At length, however, both arrived; and as every

one had been ready long ago, dancing commenced
immediately. The Prince, first of all proceeding up
to the dais at the further end of the room, while
the band played the National Anthem, opened the
ball. As for my humble self, though I had plenty
of partners, I did not by any means enjoy the slow
dances. Everybody *would* try to dance them, and
as there were just twice as many people present as
the room would comfortably hold, the result was
that wrong couples *vis-à-vised*, strange sets inter-
mingled with your own in the ladies' chains; and
as for the last figure of the Lancers, those who are
acquainted with that dance can imagine the inextri-
cable confusion into which we were thrown when
they learn that a square of planking four feet each
way, was about the allowance per set. Of course,
things were different in the Prince's neighbourhood.

Our men played till supper-time, and then the
native band (negro) requested permission to play
the march in. And a queer sort of march it was.
Such a performance I never heard before or since,
and it was with great difficulty any of us could keep
his countenance.

All things come to an end somehow, and so at
last did the abominable march. And then followed
that clatter of knives and forks and popping of
corks, which I have before alluded to as being so
grateful to the senses of the English ball-goer; and
the people of St. Kitts knew how to provide a

supper too. The noise or rather the murmur which
of course accompanies the discussion of such good
things was brought to an abrupt hush by the aide-
de-camp informing us in a stentorian voice, "that
his Excellency the Governor would propose a toast,"
which was, I need hardly add, "the Queen."
Again commenced the buzz of conversation, to be
again hushed by the announcement of a second
toast; and so we ran through the usual round of
"loyal and patriotic" health-drinking (including, of
course, that of Prince Alfred himself), one by one
subsiding into the dancing-room to have another
round or two before going off.

I should add, that before each toast was drunk, it
was prefaced by a few words from the worthy governor. As they were all of a nature which required no
oratorical flow of words to ensure their coming home
to the hearts of Englishmen, it did not much matter how they were prefaced; but should he ever rise
to address a body " of free and independent British
electors," the pages of " Enfield's Speaker," would,
I imagine, afford him some useful practical hints.

The uniform of the governor of each island was
so precisely alike, that it had engendered a belief
amongst us that the same identical coat, carefully
packed, had been forwarded from island to island, to
enable that official to appear in a becoming dress.
Either that was the case, or else the coats of some
have been made as Pat directed his to be, " as much

F

cloth as yiz convaniently can for the money;" or,
perhaps, a third idea, suggested by a messmate, may
be the cause of the bad fit—viz., that the governor
of an island, not only metaphorically, but literally,
steps into the coat and shoes of his predecessor.

We got on board about three, a.m., and on Friday,
the 22nd March, left Basseterre Roads for Tortola.

The name of St. Christopher was given to this
island by Columbus, on account of the peculiar
conformation of the mountains. "The island
having on its upper part, or, as it were, on one of
its shoulders, another lesser mountain, which gave
it some resemblance to the statues common at that
time over church porches of St. Christopher carrying
our Saviour."* But Columbus's own christian name
was Christopher, and may not this have had something to do with it? Resolved that if his surname
were not destined to descend to future generations
in conjunction with the mighty continent he discovered, that his christian name at least should be
remembered in one of the fairest isles of the windward Archipelago.

The pilot who took us into Tortola Roads anchored
us so far out that we could hardly see the apology for
a town which the island boasts. Several of the
officers landed and obtained horses for the afternoon.
For my own part, I preferred remaining on board
to attempting to get a ride on an island which

* Martin.

looked as promising in the way of " steep gradients "
as Madeira itself. I believe my estimate of the
roads was somewhat faulty, as my messmates said
they had a very good ride. However, such being
the case, a few dry facts connected with the place
will be all I shall be able to give.

Tortola is one of about fifty islands and islets
(called bays) the whole of which comprise the group
called the Virgin Islands, so named after the eleven
thousand virgins famous in Romish legends*—
those of Cologne, I presume. Like their namesakes,
they appear, with two or three exceptions, to be
barren in the extreme ; and, to carry the analogy
still further, seem to be of no particular use to any
one ; so that Columbus made a better hit than he
intended in thus naming them. Of course I exclude
from this description the islands of Tortola, St.
Thomas, and St. Croix. A few others have one or two
small hamlets on them, whose inhabitants are said
to rejoice neither in good morals nor good health.
One is named Guana, from the immense number of
that species of lizard abounding on it. I must refer
my readers to page 156 of Martin's " British
Colonies," for an account of a planter, who in 1810
was an inhabitant of Tortola, and who in a space of
three years is said to have destroyed " sixty slaves,
including women and children. Possessed with a
spirit of the most diabolical cruelty, he appears to

* Martin.

have experimentalized upon human life much in
the same manner as a chemist might have tried the
effects of poison upon animals, with no other motive
than the horrible one of inflicting the greatest
possible amount of agony on his victims." He is
stated " to have been a man of liberal education and
polished manners !" He was executed May 8th,
1811. Who would have expected to find a Cæsar
Borgia, or rather a Caligula, in such a place as this?

Amongst the fish caught by the seining parties
were several specimens of the trunk-fish, scientifi-
cally called the " Ostracion." The head and body of
this fish are covered with bony plates soldered together in such a way as to form a hard shield.
These plates are heptagonal in shape, and like those
of the turtle, which in a minor degree they resemble,
are easily separated after the fish is dead.

On the 25th March, at ten minutes after four, p.m.,
after a five hours' run, we arrived at the Danish
Island of St. Thomas, familiar to any one who has
taken passage in a West Indian mail steamer, and
no favourite with our friend, Mr. Trollope, who
expresses his dislike to it in pretty strong terms.

This island is the grand rendezvous for the English and intercolonial mail steamers, and has become
in consequence a place of some little importance.
Anything is, I believe, to be got in the town, from an
anchor to a baby-jumper. Although, as might be
expected, any amount of foreigners of all nations are

to be found in a place which presents such grand opportunities of fleecing the numerous passengers who visit it, the prevailing element seems to be English or Yankee. In fact, its lawful owners, the Danes, seem at first sight to have less to do with it than any one else.

The inhabitants told us that no fever had made its appearance there during the last three years; a statement which is contradicted by the captains of the mail packets, and still more by the people of the other islands, who, being *English* subjects, are excessively jealous of St. Thomas, a *Danish* island, being made the head-quarters of our steamers, which has, of course, greatly benefited the place, having stimulated trade and necessitated good hotels.

I have invariably found that throughout our cruise round the West Indian Islands, the place where we happened to be lying at the time was, according to the account given of it by those who lived there, the one spot which formed, as it were, an oasis of health in the fever devastated desert around it. "Fever, sir!" said a Barbadian to me; " well, we do have a *little* fever here now and then; but a mere nothing—nothing to be compared with the islands to the northward."

" Antigua ever get fever? never hear of such a thing; healthiest little island under the sun, sir. No, no; go to Barbadoes or some of those islands nearer the line if you want to see yellow fever," quoth an indignant Antigonian, to whom I put the same question.

St. Thomas is not a whit behind her neighbours in this way. It must be owned that whatever may be the true state of the case, no one out here lives as if yellow jack, like an ill-conditioned bailiff, was always prowling about the premises. In fact, there is not much danger to those who are thoroughly acclimated. Whether brandy-and-water and cigars are disinfectives I cannot say, but should imagine they were, from what I have seen of West Indian life. Perhaps they act on the " kill-or-cure" principle.

The town is a curious looking place ; it is built on three hills, nicknamed respectively Fore, Main, and Mizen tops. I am not aware how far this nautical nomenclature is carried, but on the mountain-side little white dots, said to be houses, are visible, to which elevated positions most appropriate ship terms might be applied.

The British consul invited such of the officers as landed to a party given at his house in the evening, and a very pleasant one it was, according to all accounts. I much regretted that I was not one of the lucky few who went ashore.

There is no tidal rise and fall here, so they say ; a curious circumstance, if true, as there is one at other islands lying but a very short distance from it.

When I add to the above particulars that in the

outer anchorage sharks abound, I have written all
I have to say about St. Thomas.

And now for Santa Cruz, the head-quarters of
the Danish West Indian Government.

Were I seeking some place in which I could,
without positively giving up all society whatever,
hide myself from the world and pass the remainder
of my life in almost hermit-like retirement, I would
go to Santa Cruz. Although essentially English
in language and manners, there is a Dutch quietude
reigning over the place, which an event like that of
the Prince's visit scarcely served to ruffle. Everybody seems contented and prosperous. Communication with the other islands (chiefly St. Thomas)
is kept up by a cutter or smack in fine weather, and
in foul—why, they do without it.

A party of ladies having come off to see the ship,
I accompanied them round the decks, and afterwards, with H——, went ashore. One of the gentlemen invited us to dine with him at half-past five,
and meanwhile offered us the use of his buggy to
drive round the town. There appears on this side
of the island to be no striking scenery, though some
pretty views are to be obtained. Returning to our
host's house, we dined, and then drove to the house
of Dr. S——, where, in the society of his wife,
daughters, and a few friends, we passed a most pleasant evening. We left in time to catch our boat,
being driven to the landing-place in our friend's

buggy.   I do not recollect passing a pleasanter
evening in the West Indies.

Santa Cruz is officially named St. Croix.   Why
they should adopt this plan of calling a place by
one name and writing it by another does not appear very plain.   It is always pronounced in the'
former way, which orthography I have adopted.
Frederickstadt and Christianstadt are the names of
the two towns.

I was very sorry to find on reaching the ship
that one of my messmates, W——, had fallen from
or with his horse and broken his arm.   This was
the second time he had broken the same limb, in
nearly the same place.   He had to be left behind
in charge of the Governor, who, as did every one
else, behaved in the kindest possible manner towards him.

I think I would almost have broken my arm to
have been nursed by some of the young ladies of
Frederickstadt.   As for W—— : but no ; it wont
do to tell tales out of school ; so in case this book
should fall into the hands of any of those damsels,
I shall not feel uneasy, having a proud conscious-
ness that I know how to keep a secret—*I* never
kiss and tell.

The *St. George* left Santa Cruz on the 29th
March, and on the 2nd April, 1861, arrived at the
harbour of Port Royal.   But Port Royal requires
a separate chapter.

CHAPTER V.

PORT ROYAL——JAMAICA.

THERE is scarcely, I suppose, in the Western hemi-
sphere an anchorage with which naval officers are
more familiar than that of Port Royal, or one which
more fully repays the trouble of a little inquiry
and research into its history or physical geography.
I am well aware that this latter assertion may be
rather doubted by those who, though constantly in
the habit of visiting strange places, never think it
worth their while to interest themselves in the
affairs of a " parcel of darkies." But I hope to
prove (even in the narrow limits to which I am
necessarily restricted in a work of this description)
that a history, romantic in the extreme, attaches to
the Island of Jamaica, and particularly to the town
of Port Royal, which, hovel as it now is, at one
time combined the riches of an El Dorado with the
profligacy of a Babylon.

But first of all, a few words of description. Unne-
cessary as these are to the naval man, the general

reader may take an interest in learning some particulars of the appearance of the town and harbour.

The *coup-d'œil* on entering the latter is very
striking. It was, in fact, the first thoroughly
tropical-looking place we had visited, and therefore
attracted our attention more than most other ports.
The harbour is formed by a long strip of land from
nine to twelve miles in length (according to the
person you happen to ask), running out from and
parallel with the mainland. Imagine the hill of
Portland reversed, and nearer to the coast of Dorset
than it now is, and you will have a tolerable idea of
the place, observing that Weymouth would answer
to Kingston and Portland to Port Royal.

This long sandy strip between the two towns is
called the " palisades," or " palisadoes." Why, I
have not been able to find out. On this spot all
who die at Port Royal are interred, and few places
I suppose are better known by name to the service
than the celebrated burial-ground. I shall have
more to say about the palisadoes hereafter.

A small island, forming apparently a part of the
strip, called " Gallows Point," is also celebrated as
the old place of execution for pirates. " To be
hung in chains at Port Royal," being the general
sentence on those gentry (when caught) in the
olden time.

The magnificent blue mountains 12,000 feet in
height form the background of the scene. Here

the richer inhabitants take refuge from the heats of summer. Some of the "pens," as the country residences are called, are situated in the most picturesque positions, and are visible from the ship, as little white dots on the mountain side. As of course in these elevated regions fever is an unknown visitor, all who *can* proceed thither when the sickly season sets in, leaving the town of Kingston (with the exception of a few hotel-keepers and shopmen) in the possession of the three things with which it abounds—blacks, mosquitoes, and dust.

On the 4th April a ball was given at Spanish Town, in honour of Prince Alfred's visit, to which, however, I did not go. It is a very remarkable, yet aggravating fact, that whenever I happen to stay away from anything of this sort, my messmates and friends always assure me on their return that "it was the best thing of the kind they ever saw," and so on. Such was the case on this occasion.

On the 6th the mail from England arrived, and brought intelligence of the death of Her Royal Highness the Duchess of Kent. This of course put a stop to all festivities on the Prince's behalf, so that I shall have nothing more of that sort to record for a considerable period.

The following Tuesday I went ashore, landing at De Pas' wharf; so now I will begin an account of what I saw, did, and heard of at Port Royal.

The appearance of the town when one lands is not enticing:—rather the reverse; its only redeeming features being a very first-rate hospital and a clean-looking small dockyard, in which, by the bye, our mainyard has been undergoing repairs, having been sprung in the heavy gale mentioned in the first chapter. Except the Government officials, the officers at the barracks, and one merchant, there is, I believe, not a white person in the place ;—I beg the rector's pardon, though, I forgot to include him in the exception—and I may also add, very few black ones, by which I mean that the population consists mainly of half-breeds, who look down on the pure blacks with unconcealed contempt. Some idea of the morality (or rather want of it) of this half-bred population may be gained from the remark made to me by B——, an old friend and school-fellow whom I here met : " I'll tell you what," said he ; " if the cities of the Dead Sea were *half* as bad as Port Royal in the way of morals, they richly deserved their fate."

There is a world of forcible meaning conveyed in that phrase. After talking so much about the washerwomen, I must now mention the washing. There evidently exist in different countries two separate ideas of what constitutes clean linen—viz., linen with the dirt washed *in*, and linen with the dirt washed *out*. At Port Royal, the former is evidently the correct definition. Our trousers,

smooth, glossy, and stiff, as they were on returning
from the hands of the washerwoman, presented, on
close examination, a striking likeness to that deli-
cately veined marble (Carrara, I think it is called)
which is considered so valuable for statuary pur-
poses. Our shirt-fronts were the same—starch
was used unsparingly. I have heard of their
starching an individual's sheets, but cannot speak
to that fact from personal experience, though I can
easily believe such a thing to have happened.

The English papers gave, about a year ago, long
accounts of the Jamaica revivals, and I believe the
statements they contained were received with an
almost indignant incredulity by our countrymen
at home, who, many of them, believed that these
religious orgies (for they can only be called by that
name) were indeed the workings of an awakened
faith. Far be it from me to make any remarks
which may seem to imply the slightest feeling of
disrespect for the holy religion we profess; but any
one at home cannot conceive the horrible state of
society to which these so-called revivals gave rise,
or of the awfully blasphemous language made use
of by their promoters. I do not, of course, apply
this statement to those educated and intelligent
men who really believed that the "Spirit" was
indeed working; but those who are acquainted
with the wilful impulsive nature of the black, can
easily imagine the consequences when men who

had been living lives of shameless sensuality, believing, or affecting to believe, that they were com-
missioned from on high to preach the Gospel,
rushed wildly about the streets proclaiming themselves apostles, until the excitement spreading,
two-thirds of the black population caught the in-
fection and a period of fanaticism, exemplified in
self-flagellations, &c., and language too dreadful to
be committed to paper, set in.   I have heard it
stated, on good authority, that one individual
marched through the place proclaiming that he
was our Saviour, and that a ragged troop of twelve
who followed him were his apostles.   Nor were the
weaker sex exempt from this madness; if anything,
they are said to have exceeded their male companions.   I dare not if I would, set down any of
the numerous stories I have heard, from respect to
the feelings of my readers.

"Pears to me, massa, dat dem 'revivalists' is
wuss dan we is," was the remark made to me by a
negro woman who had not joined the sect.   And
she was right.   Of course, a reaction set in; and
those who a year or two ago were held up as the
brightest examples of reformed life, are now, many
of them, so bad that they have fallen even in the
opinion of the inhabitants of Port Royal; and to
fall lower than that implies, I defy any one in the
known world.

But here I am again going off at a tangent about

affairs which, as naval officers, concerned us very
little, so must retrace my steps, and go on with my
description of the place.

My first visit was to the Palisades. After walking
about a mile on the sandy beach, covered with great
quantities of débris in the shape of brick, granite
brick and slate, evidently the remains of former
buildings, and amusing myself with picking up any
curious-looking shell or seaweed which attracted my
notice, I arrived at the set of graves nearest to the
town. They were those of men and boys who had
died last year; and though split pieces of trees with
the names rudely scratched on them did duty for
headstones, the mounds, which were all white-
washed, looked in other respects neat and trim;
and I began to think that the Palisades did not
look such a horrible place after all.

So thinking, I walked on for a short distance, and
presently found myself among the bushes, which
for the most part consisted of coffee, mangrove, and
cacti, together with the well-known "supple jack"
vine, which here grows to perfection. On turning
a corner, Heavens! what a sight presented itself.
Graves, with perhaps a dozen holes round them
(each sloping diagonally towards the coffin), inhabited by lizards and land-crabs. Tombs fallen in
or torn open, exhibiting what remained of their
ghastly occupants. Leg bones, skulls, bits of coffin,
and similar remnants of mouldering humanity, stick-

ing up here and there like badly turned-in manure.
Green lizards were rushing about, alarmed at the
unwonted footsteps.   Land crabs shuffled sideways
past one's feet, and disappeared into their loathsome
burrows.   Never before had I experienced such a
painful, sickening sensation of being " alone with
death."   Before me lay Gallows Point, previously
alluded to as the old place of execution ; at a trifling
distance, the fin of a huge shark could be seen rippling the calm surface of the harbour : all suggested
ideas of finite mortality.   Would that I had the
graphic pen of a Dickens to portray this scene !
I can assure the reader that this is no high-flown
description, composed months afterwards, when it
had been partially forgotten, but a faithful transcript
of the impressions I recorded at the time ; and even
now I shudder in describing it.

I picked up a piece of the fibula of a man's leg as
a memento of the spot, and retraced my steps, for I
had seen enough.   Had there been any living human
creature to break the awful solitude of the spot, I
might have extended my researches further; but I
was alone, and such sights are not cheerful to dwell
on in such circumstances.

Altogether, I should prefer that the Palisades
did not become my last resting-place, although,
after all, it is a matter of slight importance.   To
the visitor at Port Royal, I would decidedly say,
Don't go and see them.   The inhabitants never

do, and you had better follow their laudable example.

And now, as I stated at the beginning of this chapter that I believed the history of Port Royal to be romantic in the extreme, I shall, without further preface, extract from Mr. Martin's work an account of the town, commencing with the earthquake of 1692 :—

" Port Royal (formerly called Caguaya), five miles south-west of Kingston, and nine miles south-east of Spanish Town, stands at the extremity of a tongue of land called the Palisades, which stretches ten or twelve miles from the shore, and forms a natural breakwater for the protection of Kingston harbour, though but slightly elevated above the sea level. . . . An opulent city formerly stood near this place, which was destroyed by an earthquake. . . .

" At this period, Port Royal united to more than regal opulence the worst vices and lowest depravity which ever disgraced a seaport ; nor could anything else be expected in a city whose most honoured denizens were buccaneers—most welcome visitors, slave traders. It scarcely required the inspiration of a prophet to fortell that so much wealth and so much wickedness conjoined would have a fearful ending ; nor could any believer in a superintending Providence be astonished at the series of calamities which overwhelmed Port Royal at a time when its seeming prosperity had reached its climax. The

G

doom went forth, and a fearful earthquake engulphed
the scene of splendour and profligacy, burying in
its ruins 3000 individuals. The catastrophe was
as sudden as appalling. On the morning of the
7th June, 1692, the Governor and Council were
met in Session, the wharves were laden with the
richest merchandize, the markets and stores displayed the glittering spoils of Mexico and Peru,
and the streets were thronged with people; when
the clear and serene sky became overshadowed by
a partial darkness, broken by faint gleams of red
and purple, and a tremendous roar, like that of
distant thunder, broke from the base of the mountains, and reverberated through the valleys to the
beach, while the sea, impelled by the same mighty
convulsion, rose in a few seconds five fathoms deep
over the houses of the devoted town.

" The scene was appalling beyond description;
shrieks and lamentations rent the air; mangled
corpses floated on the waters, or were flying upwards by the violence of the shock. Although
there was no wind, billows rose and fell with such
violence, that the vessels in the harbour broke from
their moorings, and one of them, the *Swan* frigate,
was forced over the tops of the sunken houses, and
afforded a means of escape to many persons. Several
individuals were wonderfully preserved, being swallowed up during the awful convulsion, and thrown
back again through an aperture quite distinct from

that which had yawned to receive them, without receiving any material injury; of the whole 3000 houses, about 200 with the fort remained uninjured. Amidst the destruction of so much property, not the least irreparable was the loss of all official documents and records. The whole island felt the shock, and shared the disastrous effects of a visitation which happily stands alone in the history of Jamaica, no other, either before or since, having been known to compare with it. Chains of hills were riven asunder, new channels formed for the rivers; mountains dissolved with a mighty crash, burying alive the people of the adjacent valleys, whole settlements sunk into the bowels of the earth; plantations were removed *en masse*, and all the sugar-works destroyed. In fact, the whole outline was drawn afresh, and the elevation of the surface was considerably diminished.

"The sentence of desolation was, however, but partially fulfilled; a noxious miasma, generated by the shoals of putrefying bodies that floated about the harbour, or lay in heaps in the suburbs, slew thousands of the survivors. As if that so fearful a warning might not be forgotten by posterity, the sunken houses of Port Royal remain permanent memorials of Divine justice, being in calm weather still visible beneath the surface of the ocean."

From all I can see of it, the present town stands a very good chance of coming to a similar end.

G 2

The shock of an earthquake was felt about two months previous to our arrival. About the same time an American diver requested aid from the Government to explore the remains of the old city, offering also, it is said, to do his best to find the treasure said to have been contained in one of the buildings previous to its submersion. One trial was allowed him. He stated, on coming to the surface, that he had entered what was apparently a blacksmith's shop, in proof of which he brought up various pieces of iron, &c.; but reported that the fort was impracticable, it being entirely overgrown with coral, which had actually imbedded the guns in the embrasures as firmly as if they had been fixed in solid masonry. By the bye, the above account states that the fort was uninjured; a statement which, I presume, refers to the principal fortress of the place; as it is an undoubted fact that a building of this description was swallowed up, and a buoy still marks the spot, called the Fort Buoy. The *St. George* was moored some 200 fathoms further out.

"At Green Bay, on the opposite side of the harbour, is a monument commemorating the preservation of Louis Caldy, a native of Montpellier in France, who left his country on account of the revocation of the Edict of Nantes, and after having been swallowed up during the earthquake, was, by the great providence of God, flung into the sea by

the second shock, where he continued swimming
until rescued by a boat, and lived forty years afterwards.

. . . . "The colonists attempted to reconstruct
a portion of the walls of their desolated town, but
their efforts were defeated by a hurricane." Then
followed almost immediately the descent upon the
island by the French under Du Carse. The unfortunate colonists suffered, in addition to the ordinary
horrors of war, a series of diabolical tortures, which
were so bad that modern writers refuse to give particulars. Roasting alive by degrees, beginning at
the feet, appears to have been one of the mildest.

" The town at length having been partially re-
built, was in 1703 again desolated by a conflagration
which reduced all its buildings to ashes, except the
forts. Notwithstanding these calamities, and several minor ones, attempts were once more made to
restore it, and with some success ; but in 1722 the
sea broke over the breastwork, flooded the streets,
and nearly destroyed the church and houses at the
eastern end. In spite of this series of visitations,
the site gradually became covered with houses,
mostly constructed of wood. On the 13th July,
1815, a fire broke out, which in a few hours burnt
down almost the whole of the buildings, including
the Naval Hospital. No further efforts were made
to reconstruct the town ; Government purchased
part of the adjoining land, enclosed it in a high

and strong wall, and strengthened the fortifications, making it exclusively a naval and military
station." Few places, I imagine, can parallel a
history like this.

"Port Royal," according to the same author,
" now consists of five or six moderately wide streets,
traversed by lanes, in which are situated square
blocks of ill-ventilated filthy hovels, the majority
of them not deserving the name of houses. Many
of them contain only one room, in which five or
six individuals of both sexes are to be found
together in the space of little more than double
as many square feet. Furniture there is none;
and as the floor usually consists of mother earth,
dirty and damp, they are more like cellars than
human habitations."

Here I conclude my extracts from the history
of Port Royal. Do not, my dear reader, accuse
me of stealing them, for they are honestly marked
as quotations; and what more would you have?

A sad picture of humanity they present; but
the truth must be told. As a set-off to the above,
I can only say that were I ever to become an
"hospital case," there is none to which I would
sooner be sent than that of Port Royal, always, of
course, excepting the locality. It is a credit to the
man who designed it, and I may add (unlike some
similar institutions I could name) to the Government that built it.

There is a very good billiard-table in a room built within the parade enclosure, and belonging to the officers of the garrison. A notice hung upon the wall informs you that a twopence is charged per game, and requests you to put your money in the box and make a note of it on the slate. No servant, however, or other person is present to ensure this regulation being carried into effect. Possibly one is supposed to be present, but like all other negroes when not under immediate supervision, coils himself comfortably down to snooze whenever he gets a chance.

The costume of the native regiment (3rd West Indian) is very picturesque. The contrast of the colours produces a brilliant effect: it is not unlike the French zouave dress, knickerbockers, however, being substituted for their pantaloons. The men are fine, well-formed fellows, and on parade look very lions. What they might be on the field is a different matter.

A coaling wharf is situated to the left of the dock-yard, at which paddle steamers can coal. There is not, I believe, water for vessels of larger draught.

On the shore opposite to Port Royal is situated Fort Augusta, which has suffered from both fire and hurricane. In 1763, the magazine was struck by lightning; 3000 barrels of powder exploded, and 300 individuals were killed, the buildings, bastions, guns being blown to atoms.

As I now bid farewell to Port Royal,* I can assure my readers that I do so with unfeigned pleasure. This has been, I am afraid, a dull chapter, but who could create subjects for laughter from such a place as this. Such is Britain's greatest naval station in the Western Indies.

* "It is true that there is little of the luxuriance or beauty that we associate with tropical scenery here. It is a low bank of sand nearly nine miles in length, but scarcely anywhere more than a few hundred yards in breadth. * * * I found it barren enough ; but it was all strange, and to feet which for nearly two months had not felt the firm earth, even a run along the beach was exhilarating. The graceful cocoa-nut palm sprang up in groups from the water's edge, waving its feathery fronds over the rippling waves that dashed over its fibrous root. Great bushes of prickly pear and other *cacti* were growing on the low summits of the bank, covering large spaces of ground with their impenetrable masses, presenting a formidable array of spines, as did also a species of acacia that grew in thickets and single trees. All along the line of high water lay heaps of seaweeds drying in the sun, amongst which was particularly abundant a species of *padina*, closely resembling the pretty " peacock's tail" of our own shores, though less regularly beautiful ; and large fan corals, with the gelatinous flesh dried on the horny skeleton, were also thrown up on the higher beach. I found also in some abundance a coralline of a soft consistency and of a bright grass-green hue, each branch of which was terminated by a radiating tuft of slender filaments. Shells were very scarce on the beach, but on the harbour-side many species were found in the crevices and pools of the low rocks just within the margin of the water. All were small, and few presented any facts worthy of notice.—"The Palisades" : Gosse's *Naturalist in Jamaica.*

CHAPTER VI.

KINGSTON—JAMAICA.

I FEEL a positive pleasure on sitting down to commence this present chapter, to think that I have quite done with that horrible Port Royal. Not that I have much more to say in favour of the *town* of Kingston, for the simple reason that the little I saw of it was not calculated to impress a casual visitor like myself with a very favourable idea of the mercantile capital of Jamaica. But as I love fair play, considering that it may possess excellences which, like the good qualities of an Englishman, require a pretty close acquaintanceship before one is fully aware of them, I will be as sparing of criticism as of praise.

For the sum of half a dollar I and another person, name unknown, were safely conveyed from Port Royal to Kingston. You will observe that I say *safely*, thereby intimating that it was by no means a matter of course that the five miles sail should be accomplished without a capsize. Such at least was my opinion whilst in the canoe, though

I am bound to add, that accidents hardly ever occur, and that these frail—no, not frail, but unseaworthy-looking crafts, are (as I am assured) preferred by most negro boatmen to the more European-looking clinker-built boats. Fancy to yourself a canoe (or I should rather call it by its local name of "Dory") the very counterpart of the machine which through the medium of sixpenny books (sevenpence half-penny coloured) were presented to your youthful eye as that in which the adventurous Crusoe performed his voyage of discovery round his island domain. Fancy yourself, I say, in one of these, rigged with a high cotton sail, occasionally observing the lee gunwale to dip under the surface of the water, in a way which renders it necessary for your black pilot to balance himself on the weather gunwale, and so form a counterpoise to the force exerted by the wind on the large and disproportioned sail; add to this a painful knowledge of the fact that sharks—very hungry sharks—abound in the waters around you, and that against them even the best swimmer is powerless; and then, taking all these circumstances into consideration, would you not feel that you ought to be thankful for a *safe* passage? I know that I was.

Some four or five days before I visited Kingston, a couple of my brother officers were returning from the town late at night. It was very squally, and one of them was so tired that he went to sleep; the

other was unable to follow his example, the more
so as he had fears that the carelessness of the boat-
man (who did not seem to know much about his
work) might capsize them. Suddenly one of the
men in the boat directed his attention to three
comet-shaped streams of fire caused by something
following in their wake, and he shuddered when he
became aware that three enormous sharks were
keeping up with the "dory," with the evident intention of being "in at the death" in the event of
an accident. They must have afforded cheerful
subjects of speculation as to which would in that
case get first bite. On nearing the ship they disappeared. Surely in this case, "where ignorance
was bliss 'twas folly to be wise," and I should have
much preferred to be the "sleeping partner" in this
unpleasant little cruise.

Arrived at the landing-place, I took a chaise (fare
sixpence) to the "Date Tree" Hotel, rather expecting to meet some of my messmates there who I
knew were in the town. Not doing so, I sauntered
round it, and entered several shops in the vain hope
of purchasing some tobacco. I need scarcely now
inform the reader that I am a smoker, having previously mentioned cigars as objects calculated to
afford me great consolation when partners were not
to be had at any of the many balls I attended; so
do not be shocked, my dear Madam or Miss, at
my unblushing avowal that I made attempts to

purchase tobacco. Cigars were to be had in plenty,
but not an ounce of the weed could I get fit to put
in a decent pipe, and the cause I verily believe was
that every one whom I asked was *too lazy* to tell
me.

"Can you tell me, my good man, where I can
buy some tobacco?" was the query I addressed to a
large black, who was busily employed in eating a
piece of sugar-cane.

"Tobacco," he drawled out.

"Yes, tobacco; for smoking."

"Why, dere's some to be got up dere," he said,
in a tone which pretty clearly showed that he dis-
liked being questioned—(certainly it was very hot,
lazy weather, but that does not affect a negro)—
pointing with his hand up the street, but in such
an indefinite way that "up dere" might mean the
church steeple or the blue mountains in the distance.

"Well, where? Up this street? This side
of the way?"

He looked at me with a sort of sleepy stare,
grunted out "Yes; 'spose so," and resumed his attentions to the sugar-cane.

I had similar good fortune with two others I
addressed. After that I did not dare ask any
more questions. It is disagreeable to be snubbed,
even by a black man. With regard to the town, I
have bound myself over not to say too much to

its disadvantage, so will merely remark, that either there is no "Commissioner of Public Ways" in Kingston, or, if there is, that he is a very lazy personage. Possibly the laziness may be on the part of his subordinates. Whoever the cap fits, let him put it on.

But while I refrain from many remarks on the town, I conceive myself free to say what I like about the dust and the mosquitoes. As for the former, it abounded everywhere: got up one's nose, into one's eyes, and, in fact, rendered walking even a short distance as disagreeable a performance as could well be imagined; and when one fondly believed that he had escaped torment by taking refuge in a shop, those blood-sucking vermin the mosquitoes immediately began dinner at your expense, and I began to understand why no one in Kingston walks who can possibly afford to ride.

Having thus given vent to my feelings about the disagreeables I encountered, let me hasten to reverse the picture and record the hospitality I received from the few gentlemen whose acquaintance I had the good fortune to make whilst in Kingston.

Instead of returning to the "Date Tree Hall" Hotel, I entered its rival and opposite neighbour, "Barkley Hall," (and here, let me add, that whatever *unfavourable* remarks may be made of Kingston, neither of these hotels should be included in them.) Having rested therein for the space of half an hour

or so, I was just leaving when I encountered at the
door Mr. B——, a gentleman to whom I had been
introduced the previous day by one of my messmates.　He in the kindest manner insisted on my
remaining to dine with him, offering, in the first
place, to drive me round the town, and, if I had no
objection, to visit some friends of his who lived at a
short distance.

Our drive lay through the street in which is
situated St. Andrew's church, a small building,
whose only point of interest seemed to be its extreme age.　We had driven some little way past it,
when B—— suddenly observed—"By the bye,
would you like to see Benbow's tomb?"

"What, the tomb of the celebrated naval hero !
Is *he* buried here?"

"Yes; why, you don't mean to say you didn't
know that?"

"No, indeed I didn't.　All our naval histories
say he was buried in England."

"Well, come along, and we'll have a look at it."

So the horse was pulled up, and after some difficulty a boy was procured who would condescend
to hold it.　It was evidently a favour on his
part.

We were much chagrined to find that the church
door was locked, and that the sexton's house opposite was closed.　At length I suggested trying the
belfry door, which we had omitted previously, think-

Here lyeth Interred the body
of Iohn Benbow Esqr Admiral
of the White a true pattern of
English Courage who lost hys life
in defence of hys Queene and
Country   November y^e 4th 1702
in the 52nd year of hys age
by a wound in hys leg received
in an engagement with
Mons. Du Casse, being much
lamented.

ing it impossible that the sexton could be up there.

But there he was, sure enough. The door opened on our turning the handle, and we commenced ascending the stairs, as we heard some one hammering away overhead.

" Who comes dere?"

" All right; only me. I've brought a gentleman in who wants to see the church and old Benbow's tomb."

When we reached the belfry we found the sable guardian of the edifice repairing the bell (a very fine toned one, bearing date 1834.) B—— repeated his request, and the keys were produced.

As in "Deeds of Naval Daring," a deservedly popular work in the navy, and one which is to be found in all ships' libraries, it is stated that " Benbow returned to England to die of his wounds broken-hearted, tradition only pointing to Deptford churchyard as his last resting-place," I have much pleasure in being able, I believe for the first time, to give the public a drawing of his tombstone. It consists apparently of a slab of blue marble or slate in a high state of preservation; it is situated on the left hand side of the chancel, under the communion railings.

One could not help gazing with reverence at the stone beneath which lay the ashes of one of England's greatest naval worthies. It was classic ground, and his body finds a fit resting-place in the island to which he rendered such service, and in whose defence he lost his life.

On entering the church I was much struck with the *old world* appearance it presented. The various tombs and tablets were, in spite of their antiquity, in a perfect condition, and the inscriptions might have been cut just ten years, instead of one or two hundred, so sharp did they still remain. Some dated back to 1660, and many to 1700—1750. Intramural burial must have taken place to a large extent.

The tombs in the churchyard had not, however, been equally fortunate in escaping the ravages of time's destroying hand; many had fallen into a state of decay, and exhibited a very disagreeable appearance to one accustomed to the trim kept cemeteries and country churchyards of dear old England.

I noticed this to my friend B——, who replied, that the climate had a great deal to do with it ; at the same time he admitted that a little care would not be ill-bestowed.

"And talking of these old tombs," said he, "reminds me that I had a very curious document at one time in my keeping, which is now lodged in the State Paper Office—viz., the will of Sir Henry Morgan, the buccaneer, who is supposed to be also buried in this churchyard. If the office was not closed to-day I would show it to you. I think, however, that I can recollect the first few lines, which are as follows:—

"*In the name of God, Amen. Being about to depart for the Spanish Main, and being aware of the uncertainty of human life, I, Henry Morgan, Buccaneer, do hereby will and bequeath*," &c., &c., or words to that effect.

"Well," I remarked, "men in those days liked to call a spade a spade, any how." Accounts vary as to what ultimately became of this celebrated rover. Some say that he died governor of the province, enjoying the fame of being the bravest and most fortunate man of his day ; and others, that he died in prison, despised and neglected by the government to whose security he undoubtedly largely contributed.

B—— expressed great surprise at Benbow's tomb being so little visited. "I should have thought it would have been considered a sort of *Shrine* to the British navy," was his expression. But he could hardly find fault with us, as it appears that many residents in the town are not aware of its existence; and even those who *are*, manifest so little interest in it as to allow it to be almost hidden from view by cumbrous railings and pews.

Receiving the trap in an unimpaired condition from the hands of the ebony urchin, its guardian, we remounted and proceeded. As we drove through the town we frequently passed under arches of palm leaves, evergreens, &c., erected by the inhabitants in honour of the Prince. Very tastefully were many of them got up, for people of all denominations had vied in giving him a loyal reception. Well did Jamaica maintain her character of being one of the most attached appanages of the British Crown; and had not the melancholy news of the death of his august grandmother put an abrupt stop to all exhibitions of feelings of joy, to be succeeded by one of deep sympathy for his bereavement, the Prince would, I am sure, have enjoyed in no small degree the generous hospitalities of the colonists.

A three-mile drive brought us to the "Pen" of Mr. M——, the rector of the parish, who, with his wife and daughter, did everything in his power to make us feel at home. We spent a very pleasant evening in their society, and about 9.30, p.m., drove back to the town.

As the horse was rather restive, B—— very short-sighted, and the night pitch dark, it was, I suppose, a matter of congratulation that we reached the hotel all right. As we drove along, the hum of the çicada (I do not know whether my orthography is correct) broke the stillness of the night. The noise made by this insect is like the familiar chirrup of the cricket, but much louder. Its effect on a still tropical evening is rather to relieve the utter quietude of the scene, and is not to my mind

unpleasant. Myriads of fire-flies were darting about
—gleaming for an instant here, there, and everywhere. The croak of frogs swelled the chorus of
insects, and the plashing of the distant waves on
the sandy beach completed the sounds and sights
which made one realize the fact that one was within the tropics.

Of course, 10, p.m., is too late to eat a dinner.
However, we had something very like a dinner,
which we called supper, by way of reconciling the
meal to the hour. Just as we were sitting down,
I heard a noise behind me, like that of a dog
scratching at the door, and turning round beheld
a land-crab making vain efforts to scale the wall.
It was, I suppose, some waif from the larder.
B—— caught and secured it, and we then fell
into an animated discussion concerning land-crabs
in general. B—— utterly scouted the idea of
the species usually eaten, and that found in
graves, being identical. I suppose I got the idea
into my head from hearing some one suggest
that the fact of the officers of the Port Royal
garrison indulging in this dish was but an ex-
emplification of the natural law of lawful retri-
bution; as, whereas the officers feasted on crabs
up above, the crabs made a meal on the bodies
of the defunct soldiers down below. However, as
B—— was so positive on the matter, I suppose
that this idea of mutual revenge is a mistake.

If so, the poetry of this dish disappears altogether.

He furthermore informed me that these animals were fed on rice for some days previous to their being cooked; and that vegetables, not decomposed flesh, formed their ordinary bill of fare, even in a state of nature. I am very sorry that I did not try a dish of crabs while in Kingston, even were it only for the sake of adding them to my gastronomic experiences—and they embrace a wide range—from puppy dog in China, to pickled armadillo in La Plata. I have, however, come to the conclusion that the grave-crab *is* eaten, although it may not be the regular article.

After spending about an hour or so at the hotel, I returned, on B——'s pony, to the landing-place. And here, in parting from him, allow me to offer, in these pages, my most sincere thanks for his attentions. It is extremely improbable that I shall ever meet him again; so, should he ever cast eye on this record of a day at Kingston, may he rest assured that his civilities to a stranger like myself are not forgotten.

As all historical notices of any country whatever must necessarily partake largely of the character of a compilation, originality is, of course, impossible. I do not like, however, to leave Jamaica without some allusion to its history, which, as I have before remarked, reads more like a romance than a sober

compilation of facts.   I shall therefore notice one
or two circumstances connected with its early
history, merely remarking that the works to which
I am indebted for the information are those I have
mentioned in previous chapters.

Jamaica was anciently called *Xaymaca* by the
aborigines, in consequence, it is supposed, of the
abundance of wood and water found there.

The tops of the Blue Mountains were first seen
by Columbus on the 3rd May, 1494, during his
second voyage.   His first attempt at landing met
with some resistance, so he proceeded to a more
sheltered haven, of which the name is not recorded,
and there also he was opposed by the natives.   It
being positively necessary, however, to careen and
caulk his ships, he forcibly landed and succeeded
in putting them to flight, killing several.   He was
greatly aided in the engagement by a huge dog,
who, having been trained to attack human beings,
terrified the natives exceedingly, it being the first
animal of the kind they had seen.   By the bye, it is
recorded by Southey that a dog, named Bezerillo,
received, on account of his prowess, the pay of a
cross-bowman and a share and a half of prize
money (though, unless he took it out in dogs' meat,
it is difficult to imagine how he received his pay).
Columbus then took formal possession of the island,
which for eight years afterwards remained unvisited
by Europeans.

It was at the expiration of that time that Columbus, on visiting the island on his fourth and last voyage, took advantage of the superstitious feelings of the Indians by informing them that, in consequence of their refusal to supply him with provisions, the sun should become darkened for a certain time—a warning from the deity that still more wonderful signs of his displeasure might be manifested, which would result in their total destruction :—in other words, he foretold an eclipse. His words had, however, the desired effect. The same story is, I believe, told of Pizarro, nor do I see any improbability of both he and Columbus having adopted the same ruse.

The natives were treated with the greatest possible cruelty when the Spaniards became fully established in the island. They appear to have been the most civilized and gentle race of men discovered by Columbus; nor, until roused by their oppressors to retaliate, did they exhibit that implacable hatred to the whites which Spanish authors represent them to have entertained. As a specimen of the way they were treated I quote Las Casas, who wrote in 1579. "I once beheld four or five principal Indians roasted at a slow fire; and as the miserable victims poured fourth dreadful screams, which disturbed the commanding officer in his afternoon slumbers, he sent forth word that they should be strangled; but the officer on guard (I know his name, and I know his relations in Seville), would not suffer it; but, causing their mouths to be gagged that their cries might not be heard, he stirred up the fire with his own hands, and roasted them deliberately till they all expired. I saw it myself."

Sixty thousand natives perished in about sixty years. So great, indeed, became the mortality amongst them, owing to the fiendish cruelty of the colonists, that Las Casas actually proposed to import blacks from Africa, in order to relieve the wretched Indians from a bondage which soon resulted in their extirpation—singular instance of a good man's sympathies being so strongly excited for one race of people that he would even enslave another to benefit them.

In 1655, Jamaica was conquered by the British, and since that date till the emancipation of the slaves, British names have been identified with a history hardly surpassed by any for cruelty, vice, and all that disgraces the name of manhood.

In my very imperfect sketch of Port Royal I have given an account of the earthquake of 1692. Up to that date, the island had made marvellous progress in the way of population and agricultural resources, but its moral condition was deplorable in the extreme, nor did this awful calamity seem to improve it in any material degree.

But to enter into a detail of the atrocities perpe-

trated on the black population—of the vice and
immorality prevalent in the towns of the island—
or of the many insurrections attended by acts, the
recital even of which makes one's blood run cold,
would not only be a task far beyond my powers,
but would exceed the intention of these pages.
My only reason for alluding to these matters is to
show that, to the historical student, there are few
parts of the world whose modern history is more
strange or interesting than that of the West
Indies. Their position in the tropics—where, to a
northern imagination, all nature seems to have
thrown an air of gorgeousness over its productions,
animal and vegetable—the fact of their having
been the scene of the buccaneer achievements of the
worthies whose names I have already mentioned—
and also the source whence many of the founders of
our wealthiest families originally derived the riches
enjoyed by their descendants — these and many
other circumstances combine to render these islands
in the highest degree interesting to the tourist or
visitor.

. But before concluding this chapter, I would add
that it is hoped untravelled readers will not imagine
that the Jamaica of olden times is in any way similar
to the Jamaica of to-day. Far different, I am happy
to say, is now the character of the government and the
governed; and the planters and gentry of this island

have, without possessing the vices, preserved the hospitable spirit of their predecessors. Since the 28th August, 1833, slavery in every form has been officially abolished in the colonies, and while the masters have learnt humanity, the slaves have made some approach to education and civilization. Of course, no good work is ever inaugurated which does not possess some drawback, and that which has attended the abolition movement is the fact that *Quashy* will not, under any circumstances, work if he can possibly help it. Now human nature requires but little for its support in the tropics, but still that little is absolutely necessary; so our coloured brother performs most unwillingly two or three days work a week, but the moment enough has been earned to last the remaining four or five days, he sits down and indulges in that *dolce far niente* which, like that of the Maltese beggar, is Quashy's idea of perfect mundane happiness.

As to speculating how, when, or whence free labour is to be obtained, that is not my province, but the "*whence*" I imagine will not be answered by mentioning the tribes of Pongo or Ashantee.

And now, farewell to Jamaica for the present. To spend a week there in a man-of-war is delightful; a month is rather too long. But the prospect of three years (especially if at Port Royal) would be almost enough to make a man jump overboard and drown himself, or take to drowning dull care instead, in that (evil) spirit, ship's rum, till death or disgrace should finish his life or his prospects..

NOTE TO CHAPTER VI.

"Jamaica, the most valuable of the British possessions in the West Indies, has an area of 4256 square miles, of which 110,000 acres are cultivated, chiefly as sugar plantations. The principal chain of the Blue Mountains lies in the centre of the island from east to west, with so sharp a crest that in some places it is only four yards across . . . There are many small rivers, and the coast line is 500 miles long with at least 30 good harbours. The mean summer heat is 80° of Fahrenheit, that of winter 75°. The plains are often unhealthy, but the air in the mountains is salubrious. Fever has never prevailed at the elevation of 2500 feet." Somerville, *Phys. Geography*, p. 122. Coming from so high an authority, the statement as to temperature should be correct, and no doubt is, as it is confirmed by the table contained in Mr. Martin's work. But from personal experience, and all I was able to learn from inquiries made on the subject, it would seem to reach a higher average. Possibly the heat is greater at Port Royal, but I have not been able to obtain any authentic record of the height of the thermometer at this place.

"Several instances of extreme longevity amongst the coloured population are recorded. One negro died in 1834, at the age of 148 years. Other cases are also mentioned of negroes reaching the ages of 151, 130, 140 years respectively; the latter enjoying good health till within five months of his death.

"Various febrile diseases, together with dysentery, diarrhœa, rheumatism, and influenza, are the most prevalent amongst the inhabitants. Cholera has also made large inroads, being chiefly confined to the coloured race.

"Amongst the lower classes the attention of the traveller will be forcibly arrested by seeing a number of black Jews, the

colour and some other characteristics of the black race being
strangely blended with the marked profile and unmistakeable
lineaments of the Israelite."—Martin's *British Colonies*.

FIREFLIES.—"The very depth of the darkness in a tropical
forest only makes more perceptible some objects there which
shine by their own proper radiance. Here and there all around
amongst the trees and shrubs, little lights are flitting along a
few feet above the ground, which the beholder can scarcely
pursuade himself are not candles borne about by some human
inhabitant of the forest. These are fire-flies, species of the same
family as the glow-worm of our own summer evenings ; but in
many instances far exceeding it in lustre. There are other lights,
however, which surpass the brightest of these ; a red glare
dashes by with headlong rapidity along the grassy edges of the
woods, now concealed, then flaming out again, which we at once
see to be of a superior character to the sparks of the woods. This
also is the torch of an insect (the Pyrophorus noctilucus) to
which ·I shall give the English name of glowfly."—Gosse's
Naturalist in Jamaica, p. 102.

JIGGERS.—I have not, I believe, hitherto mentioned this annoying little insect. But as it is one whose acquaintance is
frequently made in these regions, the following description of it
may interest my readers.

"May 24th. About this time the Chigoe or Jigger (*Pulex
penetrans*) is· numerous and very annoying. These parasitic
fleas may be seen hopping about amongst the dust of sheds and
similar places, and the naked feet of the negroes suffer constantly
from their attacks. But even the stockings and shoes of Europeans are not proof against the insidious attacks of this tiny
flea. On several occasions I have found them ensconced in my
feet; to-day I found that one had chosen the bend of my little
toe as the scene of its domestic economy. The negroes, from
mutual practice on each other, are quick at discovering and skil-
ful in extracting them, and accordingly to one of my servant
lads I entrusted the operation. Taking my foot on his knee he
began with a sharp needle to open and widen the minute orifice
in the epidermis, between which and the cutis the swollen body
of the pregnant female had taken its place. Slowly and
cautiously the lad exposed the depredator, giving no pain and not

drawing the least drop of blood, until at length he removed the
insect uninjured. The great danger to be guarded against is
the rupture of the delicate skin of the jigger's abdomen,
stretched and attenuated as it is by the great increase of its contents. If this should occur, the nitts would escape into the
wound and produce a dreadful ulcer ; such, however, is the skill
of the sable practitioners, that it very rarely occurs. The negroes
talk of two kinds, the white and the poison jigger. Mine was
of the latter kind ; and therefore a little grease was rubbed into
the cavity after the operation. . .

    " The presence of a jigger beneath the skin during the powers
of increase, is commonly described as a titillation, rather
pleasing than painful. This does not at all agree wtih my experience.   I on no occasion felt any itching, but, as soon as
I became conscious of any sensation at all, of a dull pain with
tension, somewhat like the rising of a small boil, which increased
until the cause was removed by extraction."—Gosse's *Naturalist
in Jamaica*, pp. 177-178.

TEMPERATURE.

    I hereunder subjoin a table of the maximum and minimum
heights of the thermometer at the various places visited by the
St. George in the West Indies; it is taken from one compiled by
E. G. Bourke, Esq., R.N., midshipman, of the *St. George.*

Place.	Max.	Min.	Place.	Max.	Min.	Place.	Max.	Min.
Plymouth .	30°	28°	Guadaloupe	83°	78°	St. Thomas.	81°	70°
Barbadoes {	83°	77°	Antigua .	81°	73°	Santa Cruz.	81°	76°
	84°	75°	Montserrat.	81°	74°	Jamaica,		
St. Vincent.	81°	77°	Nevis . .	81°	75°	Observa-		
St. Lucia .	80°	77°	St. Chris- }	81°	76°	tions taken }	87°	72°
Martinique .	81°	71°	topher }			at Port }		
Dominica .	83°	73°	Tortola . .	81°	70°	Royal.		

CHAPTER VII.

GREAT INAGUA. LONG ISLAND. BERMUDA.

LEAVING Port Royal, we come to islands which will, I fear, afford but a short and a dull chapter—viz., Great Inagua, Long Island, and the Bermudas.

On the 16th April, 1861, we arrived at and anchored off Great Inagua. Our anchorage was named Man-of-war Bay, a distinctive appellation which was needless, as I should imagine that no merchantman would ever cast anchor off such an unpromising-looking place. Perhaps it is so called because no vessel *but* a man-of-war, with her large complement of men and abundant resources, could with any safety venture to use it as a haven during the prevalence of certain winds.

There is very little to be said of this island. Its chief productions are, I believe, sand, shells, and sponges ; which latter I can recommend to the commanding officers of ships as excellent substances for cleaning paintwork, as they combine the elasticity of the sponge with the roughness of the pumice-stone. The beach offers many allurements to the conchologist, as from what I saw, a careful

search would no doubt discover many specimens
which would be worth collecting. Beyond this
nothing is to be found—at least, as far as we know,
for we did not visit the town, which I have no
doubt would have welcomed us right heartily had
we done so.

It coming on to blow heavily on the 17th, we
had to weigh quickly, and during or after the operation we lost one of our bower anchors and cables.
As I am not skilled in nautical science, I cannot
offer any opinion as to how this happened, nor
would it be right of me to do so. Sufficient to say,
that it was one of those unavoidable accidents which
will sometimes happen to the best regulated ships
or families. On the 18th April, we anchored off
Long Island, a place which affords room for even
less remarks than Great Inagua. Our only amusement was fishing, several seining parties being sent
away. Amongst the fish caught, two very beautiful
species attracted my attention; one, called by the
ship's company " old maids," of a dark colour, with
bright blue streaks on the head and back, and with
a pair of jaws strong enough, apparently, to bite
through a handsaw; the other, a fish of a bright
ultramarine blue all over, named the "parrot fish."

On the 2nd May land was reported a-head, and
in a short time the outline of Ireland Island, Bermuda, became distinctly visible. Two or three
hours' run brought us sufficiently near to receive a

pilot, under whose care we steamed through the
narrow and dangerous entrance to the harbour in
safety, and soon found ourselves at anchor opposite
the dockyard.

It would be in direct opposition to all precedent
were I not to quote Shakespere's appellation of the
"Still vexed," &c., &c. I have at the present
moment three books in my possession, each of which
repeats this oft-quoted expression. I may say four,
as the Life of Moore contains a notice to the same
effect. However, it is excusable in a collection of
poems. One of the officers of the ship said to
me one day, "Well, D——, if ever you write
a history of our cruise, *do not* call Bermuda
by that hackneyed phrase, the 'Still vexed Ber-
moothes' "—a request I promised to comply with.
In fact, I myself do not see anything in the
"Tempest" to warrant the statement so commonly
made that the great dramatist intended these
islands as the scene of his play; Ariel, to the best
of my belief, merely informing his master that he
had once called him from his slumbers to perform
the somewhat troublesome job of fetching dew from
them. If Mr. Knight, or any other well read
Shakesperian commentator had only visited Bermuda in a man-of-war's gun-room, they would no
doubt have been able to accurately determine the
truth of this important question.

Anyhow, I should say that a person must be

gifted with an unusually strong poetic imagination
to realize the presence of the creations of the great
dramatist in such an unromantic spot as Ireland
island. Caliban might possibly be matched, but
such sprites as the willing Ariel have fled the spot
long ago. The society one meets (or rather their
uniform) is not cheering—blue and gold buttons,
red and ditto, and yellow turned up with burnt
sienna being the prevailing colours. When you
land, the first person you meet is, ten to one, a
sentry; a few steps further on the cheerful rig of a
convict comes in sight, closely followed, of course,
by his guard, and so they succeed each other:
convict, soldier and guard—soldier, guard and
convict, till the eye, wearied by the constant repe-
tition of the same dress, seeks in vain for a civilian
to break the monotony of colour by some variety.
Even a navvy is a welcome sight; for he suggests
the possibility of a life of which martial law, bolts
and bars do not form constituent elements.

I had often heard of the intricacy of the passage,
but was by no means prepared to see such an immense number of rocks "knocking about" the passage. By the bye, I heard a somewhat amusing
yarn about a vessel, in the good old times, before
brass topsails had partly superseded canvas ones,
while she was beating out of this tortuous entrance.

The captain of this vessel was, it appears (for in
those days there were black sheep even amongst

such exalted personages as Captains, R.N.) not altogether sober, and the ship had, mainly under the master's direction, been going about as the exigencies of the case required, when the "ruling power" came on deck and seated himself aft.

"Time to go about, sir," said the master, addressing him with the usual salute.

"Go 'bout, oh, ver' well; shpeak t'you on that shubjec t'morrow."

The master put her about, but did *not* speak about that subject next morning.

But to return for a moment to our yellow-clad acquaintances.   There is, an easy sort of style about them, notwithstanding the imposing array of soldiers and guards, which but ill accords with our home ideas of the convicted felon.   They criticise you aloud as you pass, and will, if permitted, enter into conversation with you in a way which suggests the unpleasant idea that they could master one if they chose, only they do not happen to at that precise moment.   They generally have rings, guns, and other knickknacks for sale, made of stalactite, and, although strict orders are in force prohibiting this traffic, contrive to derive a pretty lucrative trade in these matters.   Still, I believe, in spite of this apparent freedom of action, the regulations are sufficiently stringent to render any chance of escape hopeless.   Cases of mutiny are on

I

record (see "Trollope"), but have as yet always been successfully put down.

The bottom of the harbour is thickly covered with coralline growth. A favourite amusement was to lower a stout hook loaded with lead from one of the ports, and, if thrown to some little distance and dragged along the ground, it was nearly sure to detach a branch, which could then be drawn to the surface. Some very fine specimens were obtained in this way. After being taken from the water, it is necessary to boil them in alum-water, in order to destroy the animal matter and produce that white appearance which coral usually presents.

Sea-fans and a peculiar sort of seaweed which twists into capital riding-whips are the only other curiosities which the sea affords. The former are of various colours—yellow, blue, and black, and are pretty objects for the home drawing-room. The best specimens are obtained by diving. Shells are obtainable, but not in great numbers.

Our favourite bathing-place was a stone pond, or tank, within the dockyard walls, just under the Commissioner's house. By the bye, this house is a monument of building ingenuity and misapplied public money. It cost a round sum, and was, perhaps, worth the money; but ever since it has been built no Commissioner (whoever that official may be) has ever resided there. It is occasionally used as a receiving-house for the officers and ship's com-

pany of any ship which may happen to arrive
with yellow fever or other contagious disease on
board.

We always talk of *Bermuda*, but *The Bermudas* is
their correct designation, as the harbour is formed
by no less than 365 islands, a number tolerably
easy to recollect. I believe some of them, however, only do occasional duty as islands, the fall of
the tide leaving a communication between them
and the mainland; but any how, it is remarkable
that such should be the number. I do not know
who the persevering individual was who undertook
to count them, or what authority there is for the
statement, but—*Se non è vero, è ben trovato*.

It is said that only two correct charts of the
islands and their belongings—to wit, coral reefs—
are in existence, and that one is to be found at the
Hydrographer's Office at the Admiralty, and the other
among the records of the island. At all events,
some sixteen pilots are the only individuals who
are supposed to understand the mysterious passages
and turnings of the intricate entrance to the harbour, and, naturally enough, they feel themselves
men of importance. The way in which the orders,
"Port" and "Starboard," were issued by the
" coloured genelman" who piloted the *St. George*
in and out, was enough to cause the most absolute
autocrat in Europe to despair of imitating him.
He clearly felt that he was " the right man in the

right place," so we bowed to circumstances, and treated him with becoming respect.

I am afraid that this is getting a very dull chapter; but what can be made out of limestone, convicts, and Government officials?

The geological formation is calcareous sandstone, and in some parts limestone ; coral bank extending below low-water mark. The stone, of which nearly all the buildings of the dock and victualling-yards are built, seems to me, when newly cut, of a very *friable* nature, though I suppose it hardens when exposed to the air.

The islands derive their name from Juan Bermudez, who discovered them while on passage from Spain to Cuba, in a vessel named *La Garga*, having on board General Overdo, the historian of the Indies.*

I must not omit to mention the straw-plait and arrowroot for which Bermuda is so famous. The former is made in great quantities by the women of the islands, and is, I believe, much valued by the feminine creation in England. As I did not invest in this material, I cannot say, however, whether such is the case or not. Baskets, beautifully decorated with straw leaves and flowers, are also an article of manufacture, and command a high price.

I went on shore one afternoon to visit the hospital, which is not a bad one either. Next

* " History of Bermuda."

to Port Royal it is, I should say, the best on the
station.

After having chatted with some of my shipmates
who were temporary inhabitants of the building, I
and a companion sauntered back to the dockyard,
visiting the burial-ground on my way. I have seldom visited one the appearance of which was more
pleasing. A profusion of oleander, pomegranate,
and other brilliant flowering-trees, were growing
in various parts of the enclosure, which rathèr
presented the appearance of a garden than a place
of sepulture. A notice at the wicket-gate forbidding visitors to pluck the flowers, showed that some
care was bestowed on them. My companion pointed
out to me the grave of the officer who was the original of Marryat's *Captain Kearney* in his immortal
" Peter Simple." Most of the deaths recorded were,
I noticed, from accident. We left Bermuda on the
15th May, and were all, I believe, heartily glad to
see the shores of St. George's Island astern. The
Jason and *Nile* accompanied us, and it was intended
that we should proceed to Halifax, Nova Scotia, in
company.

On the passage up, we had several trials of speed.
In a light wind the *St. George* beat the *Jason* in
sailing; the latter, however, managed when the
wind freshened to cross our bows, and so fulfil their
boast of being able to " walk round us" like " a
cooper round a cask." It was a narrow shave for

her, nevertheless. We continued in company till
the evening of the 20th, when by mistaking the
light of a merchantman down to leeward for that
of the flagship, and following it, we found the *Nile*
on the morning of the 21st hull down to windward.

This day may be registered in black letter in our
diary. At an early hour the hands were turned up
to reef topsails—an operation which our men took
three-quarters of an hour to perform. Poor fellows!
I really pitied them; the cold was (we having been
accustomed for the last three months to tropical
weather) intense. B——, one of our midshipmen,
nearly fainted on coming below, and several of the
others were quite benumbed. The thermometer
fell from its average height at Bermuda (60° to 70°)
to 38°. All the decks, and the gun-room especially,
which is always peculiarly favoured when there's
any water knocking about, were ankle deep in water.
Splendid weather for ducks it might have been, but
to eat one's dinner with feet dangling in a compound
of salt water, soaked biscuit, and slops of all description, is by no means comfortable.

Next day the weather moderated, so we lowered
the screw, and proceeding under steam, reached
Halifax safely on the 22nd May.

CHAPTER VIII.

HALIFAX.

IF the reader feels as much pleasure in finishing the perusal of the last chapter as I have felt in writing its last words, he will be as glad as myself to reach the capital of Nova Scotia. The very name of Halifax is exhilarating in itself, speaking of pretty faces, fishing, shooting, picnics, and all those other pleasures which are to be found therein, and which few appreciate with greater zest than naval officers. I feel a positive delight in beginning to chronicle our doings at this place, for I have something to talk about, whereas the few materials at disposal obliged my notice of Bermuda to be uninteresting and short in the extreme.

Now, such an important subject as the town in question is not to be written on lightly. So wide a field presents itself, that it will be necessary to divide it into two or three parts; so as we shall again visit Halifax on our cruise, I shall reserve the discussion of the above-mentioned pretty faces and field-sports for our second visit.

Of course, the Prince went to Government House ;
but in consequence of the Royal family's recent
bereavement, there was no public landing, greatly,
I imagine, to the disappointment of the good people
of Halifax.

The first affair of any interest which took place
after our arrival was a race between two cutters,
belonging respectively to the *Nile* and *St. George*,
manned by their gun-room officers. The following
notice, which appeared in *Bell's Life*, will give a
tolerably fair idea of the race :—

"*Sunday, August* 11, 1861.

" BOAT-RACING AT HALIFAX.

" Within the last few weeks the naval forces
stationed at this capital have been in a state of
great excitement (not altogether unshared by the
inhabitants) on the subject of boat-racing. H.M.'s
ships *Nile* and *St. George* (both of which possess,
perhaps, the best racing crews in H.M.'s navy) had
agreed that a trial of their respective boats should
come off on the 30th May last. The race was won
by the cutter of the *St. George*, both crews pulling
a very long race in the most creditable manner.
Anxious to redeem their character as the crack
racing ship of the station, the *Nile's* gun-room
officers challenged those of the *St. George* to a

second trial of speed on Thursday, June 6. The
morning of the 6th promised a pleasant day for the
race, which promise was fulfilled. About half-past
four, the rigging of the *St. George, Nile, Racer*, and
Pyramis might be observed to become gradually
crowded with a dense mass of maritime humanity,
the more excited among the blue jackets ascending
to the topgallant rigging. About ten minutes to
five, both boats came to the starting-points, and a
stranger had for the first time an opportunity of
observing the condition and training of the respective crews. Three or four in each boat were naval
cadets, making up in zeal what they wanted in
muscle, each of whom was evidently determined
that no effort on his part should be wanting to win
the race for his own boat. The crew of the *Nile's*
boat gave the idea of the greatest physical strength.
Lord Albert Clinton, naval cadet, was coxswain of
the *Nile's* cutter; and Mr. P. B. Aitkens, naval
cadet, of the *St. George's* (the latter in the place of
His Royal Highness Prince Alfred, who was on
leave at Quebec at the time, or would otherwise
have been coxswain of the boat). The course lay
round two buoys, which compelled the boats to
describe a sort of oval between their starts from and
return to the winning boat. At length, at ten
minutes past five, the gun was fired, and off they
went, the *Nile's* boat shooting ahead with an im-

petus which for some minutes gave them a decided
lead. They continued ahead till the two boats
came almost abeam of the *St. George*, when a tremendous cheer from that ship seemed to have put
sudden spirit into the crew of her boat, and half a
dozen vigorous strokes brought them even with, or
slightly ahead of the *Nile's* cutter. Neck and neck
they pulled towards the buoy, and as it was evident
that whoever passed the buoy first to turn would
have by far the advantage, the excitement was at
this moment excessive. Presently the *St. George's*
began to draw slightly ahead, the distance gradually
increased, and at length a thundering cheer from
the crews of the nearest ships proclaimed that she
had passed the buoy first. From this moment she
never lost her lead; though urged by desperation to
almost superhuman efforts, and though the *Nile's*
crew did all that bone and muscle could do to re-
trieve their position, it was a lost game for them.
As the boats passed under the stern of the *St. George*,
the band struck up, 'See the conquering hero comes,'
followed by 'Cheer, boys, cheer,' for the *Nile's*. In
the evening a supper, to which all the officers of
both ships were invited, finished up the day, and
effectually dissipated any sore feeling which might
have existed on the part of the losers of the race
—viz., the officers of the *Nile*. The boats' crews
were :—

NILE.		ST. GEORGE.	
Port.	*Starboard.*	*Port.*	*Starboard.*
Liardet.	St. Clare.	Walters.	Bruce.
Ballantyne.	Forder.	Hon.H.G.P.	
Bell.	Medder.	Meade.	Johnstone.
Mallony.	Boddam.	Mandeville.	Grey.
Boteler.	Otter.	Goldson.	Hon. E. S. Dawson.
Lord A. Clinton (cox.)		Nesham.	Talbot.
		P. B. Aitkens (cox.)"	

So much for the newspaper account. Our men were so exultant at the result of the race, that they pulled round the *Nile* with a cock in the bows of their boat, thereby exasperating her crew to a great extent. It was an ill-judged proceeding, but pardonable in the first flush of victory, and fortunately led to no disturbance, the officers of both ships having too much good sense to allow the "*tarroos*" to carry out their own ideas of maintaining the honour of their respective ships.

Now those who have read the above account will notice that, according to the "sporting correspondent," "a supper . . . finished up the day, and effectually dissipated any ill feeling," &c. &c. So it did; but—"thereby hangs a tale."

After the race was over, every one interested in the day's proceedings went ashore; and by way of passing the time, dropped into Temperance Hall to hear a performance given by Rumsey and New-

come's Minstrels. One part of the affair attracted
special approbation. The bills announced that
Mr. —— would perform a solo on the trumpet.
So, when a large cornet-à-piston box was produced,
all eyes expected an orthodox brass instrument to
make its appearance therefrom. But we were sold;
for amidst roars of laughter the performer produced
a *penny trumpet*, such as one buys at a toy stall,
and in the gravest manner possible proceeded to
play an overture, accompanied by the double bass
and big drum; and a better performance I have
seldom heard. How he managed to produce the
sound is a mystery. But certain it is that the
" trumpet solo" " brought the house down."

The performance over, the officers of the two
ships betook themselves to the " Halifax" Hotel to
supper.

And now comes the little circumstance above
alluded to.

Fancy to yourselves forty naval officers after a
capital supper, with punch, champagne, &c., to match.

Fancy to yourselves the said individuals being
all under the age of one or two and twenty, and
each and all possessing a keen relish for a practical joke.

And now fancy the consequence. Here it is,
according to the Halifax daily paper :—

" ANOTHER SECESSION ACT.—On Thursday night,
a number of midshipmen belonging to H.M.S.

——, now in the harbour, were on shore enjoying themselves in a not very orderly style. In their peregrinations through the streets, they observed a dazzling object on Victoria buildings, which proved to be the sign of the American Consulate in this city. It is not to be supposed that these youngsters wished to show their contempt for the American Eagle, but true it is that their love of what they considered fun predominated over their high respect for the arms of the United States, and they removed it to one of the wharves. Six watchmen succeeded in capturing *three* of the depredators, not, however, until one of the former was pretty severely handled. They were taken to the station, and brought up before his Worship the Mayor yesterday morning, when they were fined twenty dollars each, and ordered to make good the damage done. The Mayor deserves much credit for dealing thus summarily with the case."

Now the fact is, that there lives at Halifax an ill-advised individual, whose mission in life is apparently to present temptation to junior naval officers. He is the owner of a good-sized image, which is supposed to be that of a naval officer in full dress, but which is, in truth, a libellous representation of that useful and honourable public servant. He bears a strong resemblance to the celebrated midshipman mentioned in "Dombey and Son." Naturally enough, a strong desire has existed

for many months in the breasts of the juniors of
the station to degrade this image; and after the
supper above alluded to, some three or four from
both ships sallied forth, for the purpose of displacing
him. But the fates were adverse. Cunning workmen had fixed the figure so firmly in the brickwork,
by means of iron clamps, that no effort of skill or
strength could avail to start it, so a retreat was
effected in good order. It appears that the peaceful
inhabitants were aware that there was to be a naval
supper that night, so they had stationed extra
watchmen to look after their signs; for Halifax not
only boasts a wooden naval officer, but a gutta-
percha tooth, and a brick boot likewise, all of which
were, in the opinion of every gunroom mess in the
squadron, lawful *spolia opima*, if get-at-able.

Well, the wooden midshipman not being inclined
to quit his lodgings that night, at all events, his
persecutors had to leave him in peace, and proceed
on their way (by no means rejoicing). Now it so
happened that the attention of one of them was
attracted by a large species of bird, of a nondescript kind, fixed over the door of a house in one of
the principal streets. Opinions were divided as to his
genus, some asserting that he was a goose, and others
a phœnix. To decide the point, one of the number,
Paddy M——, climbed up the verandah; and after
breaking his own head, and a pane or two of glass,
while performing his mission, succeeded in detaching

one of the wings, which was safely brought to the ground. This, however, did not satisfy the committee of inquiry; so it was voted, *nem. con.*, to dislodge the remainder of the body, which was now authoritatively determined to be that of a phœnix, the house being supposed to be a chemist's shop.

Paddy safely accomplished his task; and the body and wings lay in inglorious posture in the gutter, ready to be carried whither his captors chose. I believe that some hazy idea of a burial with funeral honours flitted across their minds as they proceeded to hoist the strange-looking bird on their shoulders, and bear him away in triumph; but all such ideas were immediately dispelled by the unwelcome appearance of some watchmen at the corner of a street. Flight was useless, but attempted; and in spite of a hard run, three of the depredators, and the eagle (which they now to their amazement discovered it to be), were captured, and they were locked up.

The upshot of the affair was as described in the newspaper; but had it not been the American eagle, I verily believe that the sympathy of the worthy Mayor would almost have been with the midshipmen. The American Consul behaved very kindly, saying that he was quite sure that the eagle had been displaced in perfect ignorance of what it really was. However, thanks to one of the bench, the

midshipmen were fined, and, worse still, had their
leave, &c., stopped when they got on board again.

I must now introduce my readers to Michael
Thomas.   Michael is a man with an abundance of
long black hair, high cheek bones, &c. &c.,—in
fact, a civilized Mic-mac Indian.   He knows every
lake and stream in the neighbourhood, and is a useful assistant when out fishing or shooting.   He has,
to the best of my belief, only one weakness—at least,
I mean a serious one (he is rather dirty, but that is
" human natur' " in an Indian), and that is being
constantly short of tobacco.   Give Mike a pipeful
one minute and ask him thirty seconds afterwards if
he has any, and he will say " No, sar," with as
innocent and unruffled a face as possible.   Mike's
chief trade is in moccasin and quill work, which
his wife and daughter work for him.   His squaw
is by no means a specimen of female beauty, and is
dirtier than her husband ; for he, I believe, does so
far forget himself sometimes as to wash his face ;
but she never does, judging by appearances.   Their
daughter, Adelaide, is a tolerably good-looking girl
(for an Indian), but takes after her mother.   I was
very anxious to find out what sort of language
the Mic-mac might be, and accordingly entered
Mike's wigwam one afternoon to try and get hold
of a few words.   The exhibition of any interest in
such a subject as their native language raised me
greatly in the estimation of the fair (?) Adelaide,

who tried to teach me a few words.   As far as I could learn, they bore no analogy to any of the same meaning in the Semitic languages.   The following may be amusing to my readers.   They were taken, not from the lips of the squaw, but from the pages of a Mic-mac breviary, kindly given to me by the Rev. Father Giroir, Bishop of Arichat, whose name will again occur in a future page.

PENOBSCOT.

KEZOGMOMNA ALAIAMIHOT.—(LORD'S PRAYER.)

K'mitangsena, Spomkik eyon wéweselmoquotch eliwisian amante neghe petsiwewitawekssane ketepeltamohanganeck eli kiklanguak ketletamohangan.   Spomkik tali yo nampikik petchikiktanguatetcho mamiline yo pemighisgak etaskiskue n'taponmena yopahatchi aneheldamawihek kessi kakanwihiolek'pan eli nyona kisi aneheldamahokit kekanwiak'tepanik musak ketali tchi kiktawighik tamambautchi saghihunmihinam'ke ulahamist'ke saghehusuhamine mematchikil.   Nialetch.

DAYS OF THE WEEK.—(MIC-MAC.)

Sunday—Kegueundiewink.
Monday—Amsgueèlugudink.
Tuesday—Taboòweèjelugudink.
Wednesday—Sistewejeelugudink.
Thursday—Neuwejeèlugudink.
Friday—Klutchieuwei.
Saturday—Ketowagandiewink.

K

MONTHS OF THE YEAR AND SIGNIFICATIONS.

January—Onglusamwessit (it is very hard to get a living).

February—Saquas'nikizoos (moon in which there is crust on the snow).

March—Pnhadamivekizoss (moon in which the hens lay).

April—Amusswikizoss (moon in which we catch fish).

May—Kikkaikizoos (moon in which we sow).

June—Muskoskikizoos (moon in which we catch young seals).

July—Atchittaikizoos (moon in which the berries are ripe).

August—Wikkaikizoos (moon in which there is a heap of eels on the sand).

September—Montchewadokkikizoos (moon in which there are herds of mooses, bears, &c.)

October—Assebaskwatts (there is ice on the borders).

November—Abonomhsswikizoos (moon in which the frost-fish comes).

December—Ketchikizoos (the long moon).

The wigwams used by the half-civilized Indians of the neighbourhood are constructed of birch bark, which possesses a variety of useful qualities. Canoes, paper, baskets, chair bottoms, boxes, &c., are made from this substance. The paper is one of the thin layers between the outer and inner skin, and will bear writing on without running.

The wigwams are floored by a quantity of pine cuttings; the fragrant smell of the resinous branches is rather pleasant. They form a capital couch with the addition of a rug, far pleasanter than straw or grass.

We left Halifax on the 22nd of June for a cruise round Cape Breton Island. His Royal Highness Prince Alfred had meanwhile proceeded overland to Quebec; the *St. George* being detained at Halifax in consequence of the unsettled state of American affairs. We were much disappointed at not being able to ascend the St. Lawrence in the *St. George*, as we had set our hearts on a trip to Niagara; but circumstances obliged us to forego this pleasure.

As we steamed out of the harbour with our band playing on the poop, hundreds of people assembled on the wharves and piers, who loudly cheered us as we passed them. In an hour's time we had passed Sambro Light and were making the best of our way to Arichat.

CHAPTER IX.

ARICHAT AND LOUISBURG TO SYDNEY.

WE arrived at Arichat on the 24th of June, 1861. The town is not striking when viewed from the anchorage, the most prominent objects, or rather buildings, being the monastery and church, both of wood, and situated on the top of a hill immediately opposite the anchorage. The Rev. Father Giroir, who is the priest of the district, came off to the ship in company with some other gentlemen, and while on board expressed a great desire to hear some guns fired. It did so happen that it was intended to go to night quarters that evening for the purpose of exercise, and the Rev. gentleman's wish was accordingly gratified. At a late hour two broad-sides were fired, which not only considerably astonished the inhabitants, but also broke a few of the windows in the neighbourhood. Our visitors expressed themselves in the highest degree delighted.

For my own part, I detest hearing guns fired (for exercise) if obliged to be too near them ; and while the Rev. Father G. and his friends were indulging in their expressions of delight, I was longing to bury my head in a blanket or some other non-conductor of sound. Verily, *tastes differ*. Father G. very kindly gave me the breviary mentioned in a former page. It is, I believe, a curiosity in its way, and contains twelve lines of a language which is, save the lines in question, totally extinct.

This was the first time that a line-of-battle ship had anchored in the Bay within the memory of the " oldest inhabitant." Of course, as usual, those who landed were received with every hospitality as far as the scanty resources of the place admitted ; but as I did not, I cannot describe either the civilities rendered or the appearance of the town when viewed at close quarters.

The inmates of the convent came off to see the ship, under the charge of two of the Sisters. Most of the young females who live in the convent are simply there for the purpose of education.

The *St. George* left Arichat on the morning of the 29th June, and arrived at Louisburg in the evening of the same day. This was at one time an important town, with strong fortifications. Being taken, however, by us during the old French war, the batteries were razed to the ground, and the town placed under the same sentence of depopulation (so pathetically described by Longfellow in his " Evangeline ") as Grand Pré and other

neighbouring towns. The following extract from
the *Cape Breton News* of 6th July, 1861, will give
a better idea of the ship's appearance in this harbour
than I can.

" Cape Breton has been privileged, during the
past ten days, to hail the arrival in several of its
chief harbours of that splendid line-of-battle ship,
the *St. George*, mounting 91 guns, under the command of Captain Egerton. This is decidedly the
largest of Her Majesty's ships of war which has at
any period visited our waters. Thursday week, the
St. George was at Arichat, to the delight and gratifi-
cation of the inhabitants of our sister town. On
Saturday last, she entered the noble harbour of the
famed city of Louisburg, now—like another Tyre
or Palmyra—stripped of its ancient magnificence.
The circumstance of her arrival there is adverted
to in a note from a gentleman, then on a visit
thither, since his return to town on Wednesday
last, and an extract from which we here subjoin :—

" ' I was surprised and delighted, on Saturday
evening last, upon reaching Louisburg, to see the
usually quiet harbour occupied by one of our noble
line-of-battle ships. The *St. George* had arrived
there a short time before, and now lay at anchor at
no great distance from the ruins of the Old Town,
—the usual anchorage for ships. It is pleasant to
see any of the ships of our gallant navy at any
time in these waters ; but as this was the first

time that I had had an opportunity of witnessing
such a sight in the harbour of Louisburg, I could
not help being struck with it. Independently of
the grand appearance which she made, from her
own noble proportions, and the formidable battery
of ninety-one guns which armed her sides,—she
afforded peculiar interest from the associations thus
awakened with former scenes in this very harbour ;
and the imagination was assisted in picturing the
life and activity which once distinguished this
famous spot. The tall masts lay upon the ruins
of the deserted city, which formed a desolate background. The grass-covered mounds and ruined
arches of this once celebrated fortress seemed to
speak of the sad chances of war ; whilst at the
same time I could not avoid a feeling of security,
in contemplating such means of protection which
our country enjoyed,—as that which there lay at
anchor before me. The evening was misty and
soft, and the fine band upon her deck was "dis-
coursing sweet music,"—which came mellowed over
the water from that distance, so as to be quite a
treat to listen to. Whilst walking the following
morning over the quiet roads, which surround the
harbour, the National Anthem struck up about
eight o'clock, with magical effect, and recalled to
my thoughts the well-known saying, that "the
beat of the British drum follows the sun in his
circling hours round the globe." Several gentle-

men visited the ship and returned much gratified with their reception and with all they had seen on board. She left Louisburg for Sydney about eleven o'clock on Wednesday morning.'

"About sunset on Wednesday, this beautiful ship came up Sydney River, under steam, against light airs of westerly wind, and anchored abreast the town. Immediately after dropping anchor the band on board the *St. George* played the French National Anthem. At eight o'clock next morning, the tri-colour of France was hoisted at the fore, and saluted ; and ere the dying echo of the guns has ceased, the band of the *St. George* struck up *Partant pour la Syrie.* The effect of the whole was most pleasing. The French National Anthem concluded, up went the Ensign of Old England at the fore on board the French frigate *Pomone,* lying about 300 yards from the *St. George,* and which was likewise duly saluted. Again at twelve o'clock, noon, as J. Bourinot, Esq., who had been on board to pay his respects to the commander, left the side of the *St. George,* her guns belched forth a salute due to the rank and dignity of a Consul of *la belle France.* During the day, parties of ladies and gentlemen were conveyed from the shore to the *St. George* in her boats, and who were cordially welcomed and conducted throughout her interior, to see and note the wonderful ingenuity that had converted this floating ship into habitations for

800 souls, besides the reserved spaces for imple-
ments of war, &c. Throughout that day and
yesterday, the officers and men of the *St. George*
have been enjoying themselves as well as the limited
capabilities of our town would permit.

"She will sail on Monday, we learn, for a port
in the Gulf of St. Lawrence, to take up Prince
Albert; and we sincerely desire that she and all
on board, with her precious freight, may reach in
safety the pleasant shores of ' Merrie England.'"

Bayonets, shot, and old coins are said to reward
the patient digger around the environs of Louisburg. An old wall is the sole remaining vestige of
this once important place. .

Some of our midshipmen landed and created great
consternation in the breasts of the inhabitants
(which are about forty or fifty in all) by chasing
their cattle and pigs; the American and French
officers who visit the place being, as they stated, in
the habit of appropriating any stray waifs in the
shape of pigs or poultry. However, we managed
to reassure them, and were soon the best of friends.

Colonel D——, who had landed to try his luck at
fishing, returned in the evening and gave a not very
cheering account of the sport he obtained. The
average weight was, he said, from two to five penny-
weights per fish! Notwithstanding his chaff, however, some of both messes landed and succeeded in
obtaining some very respectably-sized dishes full.

We left Louisburg on the 3rd July, and arrived at Sydney, Cape Breton Island, in the evening of the same day.

Next day, about thirty of the principal inhabitants came off to the ship. We had the band up on the maindeck, and got up a few impromptu dances, which apparently greatly pleased our visitors. Judge D. invited us to a dance at his house in the evening to meet the French Commodore (of the *Pomone* frigate) and some of his officers.

We took with us four of our bandsmen. As usual, when *wanted* to play well; they did not, but kept both bad time and tune. I am rather afraid that the hospitality of our hosts had something to do with it, as I noticed a good many glasses of ale disappear down their thirsty throats. However, we managed very well on the whole, and took our leave about three, a.m.

It was settled that we were to have a picnic and "*high tea*" next day; so about three o'clock in the afternoon, those of us who chose to go, landed and found a large party in readiness. Our own launch and commander's gig, together with a boat from the "*Pomone*," were in readiness at the French Consul's wharf. As there were more ladies than gentlemen, we were obliged to distribute our attentions in an impartial manner all round, which we did to *our* entire satisfaction, if not to that of our lady friends. Our destination was a pretty little cove on the oppo-

site side of the harbour, which we reached in about
twenty minutes sail. We disembarked as well as we
could ; the ladies (to their great annoyance, no doubt)
being obliged to show their ankles and jump from
the bows of the launch, as the water was too shallow
to admit of our getting very close in.

Then while some remained to prepare the *high tea*,
the remainder of us strolled about and amused ourselves in various ways. We had brought six of our
band, who tuned up in good style, and though long
grass is not a good dancing floor, we managed to
get through a few slow dances. Then came the tea,
and *such* a tea. Imagine breakfast, lunch, dinner,
and tea combined, and you will have an idea of our
meal. After a few songs, which included one or two
very good ones from our French naval friends, we
re-embarked, and, alternately pulling and singing,
managed in about two hours' time to pull a mile-and-
three-quarters—the distance back to the landing-
place. After spending an hour or two at the house
of our hospitable host, we came off very well pleased
with our day's pleasure.

Cape Breton is geographically, I believe, pretty
nearly the antipodes of Australia, and there is a
curious feature of society which renders it socially
so. According to popular report, the Australian
settlers all want wives, or at least eligible parties
who may become wives. The Cape Breton colonists,
on the contrary, suffer from a scarcity of young men,

and the poor young ladies of the present generation
seem doomed to pass the rest of their days in in-
voluntary celibacy. Poor things ! we really felt sorry
that we had not previously heard of this unhappy
state of affairs, and devoted our energies to coloni-
zing Cape Breton, instead of tempting the dangers
of the deep.

A lady friend lent me a book which had lately
appeared, and was making some sensation in the
neighbourhood. It is called " *Voyage à Terre-neuve*,"
and is the production of M. le Comte Gobineau,
one of the late Commissioners appointed by the
French Government to confer on the fishery question
in Newfoundland.   The Count did not appear to be
a favourite with our friends at Sydney, and I suppose
that the reason why may be found in the following
expression of his opinion relative to the ladies of
the neighbourhood.

After describing a ball given on board the vessel
which conveyed the commissioners, he says :—

"*Les jeunes demoiselles, douées heureusement de cet
appétit surprenant, signe charactéristique de la race
Anglo-Saxanne, ne se montraient pas moins disposées
à bien accueiller ces offrandes, et dans les intervalles
très courts de repos qu'elles permettaient à l'orchestre de
leur accorder, elles reprenaient beaucoup de forces.*"

Our friends above mentioned were among the
jeunes demoiselles herein alluded to, and were extremely indignant at having the appetites with

which nature had endowed them thus sarcastically commented on.

The Count's views of the feeling amongst the poorer population, however, is, I am afraid, but too correct. Were it an American instead of a Frenchman who had thus written, I should have imagined that he was throwing out a hint towards annexation. But certain it is, that from the infrequency of a visit from an English vessel, and the fact of its being the head-quarters of a French naval station, Sydney is becoming French in tone and feeling. I do not by any means mean to say that its loyalty is to be for a moment questioned; but I am sure that English naval officers are at a disadvantage when they visit the port, because their acquaintance with the people is that only of a day, whereas our Gallic neighbours have friends of long standing in the neighbourhood. Perhaps, as far as the society goes, it does not much matter, as there are but few families constituting it; but from the important position of the island in a geographical point of view, in relation to Canada and Nova Scotia, it may be worth while to bring the question under the notice of those with whom lies the remedy.

I cannot bid farewell to Sydney without giving my readers a copy of an advertisement which I have cut out of the *Cape Breton News*. It quite soars beyond the ideas of a Holloway or Maccassar. Here it is :—

"SPECIAL NOTICES.—Obadiah Dix, of Shute's
Falls, Tioga county, Pennsylvania, substantially
states: He has been a painful invalid for three years;
had *rheumatism*, which, serving him as it does thousands more, filled his limbs with anguish, sometimes tolerable and anon utterly intolerable; resided
in those members chiefly, but more than once did
travel to the region of his heart; a fearful visitor
is rheumatism there, thinks Obadiah, which brings
its victims face to face with the inevitable hour!
Subtle rheumatic distemper in his legs made them
worthless for locomotion—good only for torment,
unutterable pain. Assiduous care and skill medi-
cinal brought him some occasional relief; but
chiefly clouds of woe overshadowed all the sky.
One lucky day he finds a travelled friend of medical
acquirements, who tells how AYER'S PILLS are
made; their searching properties, that seize upon
disease and drag it from its strongholds; their
virtues and their cures—points to a star of hope,
does Medicus, that glimmers through the gloom on
Obadiah. Pills, procured and swallowed, purge out
the angry humours of the blood, and with them
their whole infernal retinue of ills. The Augean
stable cleansed, and foul obstructions in the blood
cast out, the vital forces then resume their wonted
action. Obadiah's legs turn dutiful again—walk,
and even run at his command, with Obadiah on
them; but bring him messages of rending pain

no more. Dreadful distemper gone! Health takes possession of her own, and from the downward swift-surging river to destruction, where, oarless and rudderless he rode, our great remedial turns him upon the placid stream of Health's perpetual spring. Obadiah mentions that he took three boxes and paid six shillings for them, and that some pills are sold at Shute's Falls for less. O worldly-minded Obadiah, that saves his life for shillings, and then revolves the cost! Is it too dear? We know not, for we know not Obadiah; but we have his well-authenticated certificate covering two letter sheets with prolix details, too much diluted for our space here. He must excuse us for this concentration."

On the 9th July, we left Sydney; it was intended to have touched at Margaree (a place which boasts the finest salmon stream in the province), but owing to our delay in sailing, on account of unfavourable winds, we did not go there. So Port Hood was the next place where we dropped anchor. On the 13th, we again weighed and steamed over to Charlotte Town, Prince Edward's Island. It had been arranged that the Prince and Major Cowell should meet at this place, and both the *St. George* and the steamer conveying them arrived within twenty minutes of each other. The Prince, however, proceeded up to Charlotte Town, where he remained till the 16th, and on that day

embarked on board us with Lady Mulgrave, who
was returning to Nova Scotia from a stay in the
island.

A very few hours saw us snugly anchored off Pictou,
when the Prince and Lady Mulgrave landed. We
were rather disappointed to find that we were lying
nearly seven miles from the town, as that distance
is rather too long to enjoy the passage in a ship's
boat if the weather is at all rough.

Before breakfast was finished next morning, we
were considerably astonished to find a steamer
alongside, and a bevy of ladies under the convoy of
Mr. P—— and his daughter, former acquaintances
of ours, boarding us, and taking possession of our
upper deck. They apologized for putting in so
early an appearance ; but said that, knowing there
would be no other chance of visiting the ship
(which was to them a sight as rare as the *Great
Eastern* to us at home), they had ventured to come,
&c., &c. Naval officers do not generally object to
having ladies on board (in harbour), so we did not
feel particularly sorry to see them. They had a
good look round the ship, and pressed us to accompany them on shore in the steamer, and several of
us yielded to their persuasion, and did so.

The Prince had meantime gone to visit the coal
mines, for which Pictou is celebrated—this town
being, in fact, the Newcastle of Nova Scotia. It
was said that a part of them was on fire at the time

of the Prince's visit, being separated from the open workings by a thick wall. As no one else visited the mines, however, our information regarding them was but scanty.

Pictou is a much larger and better built town than one would expect to find in such an out-of-the-way corner of the world. It boasts one or two decent inns, a lodge of Freemasons, &c. We had a dance in the evening at our friend's house, and came back in a boat under sail, at two shillings per head—not a dear fare for seven miles.

We took our departure from Pictou on the 18th July, the Prince having re-embarked. That night we anchored in Habitans Bay, having steamed through the Gut of Kanso, the strait of which divides Cape Breton from Nova Scotia. Before the invention of the submarine telegraph, the wire was carried from a hill on the one side to a mast on the other, at an elevation of 260 feet above the sea level, which would have permitted the *St: George* to pass underneath with all her masts standing.

On the 23rd July, the *St. George* anchored in Halifax Harbour.

L

CHAPTER X.

HALIFAX.—BALLS AND THEATRICALS.

On the day of our arrival, Prince Napoleon,
husband of the Princess Clotilde, visited Prince
Alfred on board the *St. George*. He came alongside in a steam-gig, one of the prettiest little
steamers I ever saw. After leaving the ship the
machinery, however, broke down, and we had to
send one of our boats to her assistance.

A few days afterwards an attempt was made to
take a photograph of all the officers on board in
one group; but owing to the unsteadiness of the
camera, the likenesses were indifferent, most of the
faces being very indistinct.

On the 1st of July, the Halifax Yacht Club Re-
gatta came off. Of course all our interest lay in
the matches in which our own boats took part, viz.
the man-of-war races. The *Nile* and *St. George*
were the chief opponents. The *Nile* won three
races (viz., pinnace, launch, and galley) fairly. We
won two—Commander's gig, and pinnace manned

by Marines; but the cutter's run was disputed.
The case was this. Our cutter pulled the correct
course and came in second; the *Nile's* boat pulled
a somewhat longer, but easier and decidedly irregular course, and came in first. Our boat's crew
claimed the prize, on the ground of having pulled
round the course, which the *Nile's* cutter had not,
so a pretty row ensued. The case was ultimately
referred to a committee of arbitration, which
awarded us the prize; but it required all the
influence of the officers of the respective ships, who
had too much good sense to quarrel on so trifling a
ground, to prevent the crews from settling the
question by main force. However, in a short time
the affair blew over, and no ill feeling existed
between us.

On the 7th August, the Commander-in-Chief and
the officers of the *Nile* gave a ball to the officers of
the French vessels of war laying in the harbour.
The ball-room, which consisted of the upper deck
abaft the funnel, and the poop, was capitally
decorated. At least two hundred persons must
have been present, including the French officers.
It seems to me that Englishmen always want the
tact which Frenchmen possess in making their
guests comfortable on occasions of this kind. The
unfortunate Frenchmen were to be seen, for the
most part, standing in disconsolate groups of four
or five, gazing wistfully at the girls, to whom no

one was to be found to introduce them, and evidently of opinion that the whole affair was remarkably slow. Many of them with whom I was
well acquainted, asked me to introduce them to
partners, and I was obliged to assure them that I
was in as bad a plight as they were:—barring the
fact that I was an Englishman. However, I
managed to get about fourteen dances out of the
twenty-one, and to preserve a contented mind.
When the dancing was over, we adjourned to the
gun-room, and after a few songs and toasts, returned to our respective ships and houses.

On the 9th August, Prince Alfred and Major
Cowell left Halifax by the mail steamer, for England, the former having been granted six weeks'
leave.

On the 15th, the officers of the *St. George* gave a
Bonnet Hop, of which the subjoined account in the
daily paper will give a good idea :—

" H.M. Ship St. George.—The officers of H.M.S.
St. George entertained a large party on board their
splendid ship, yesterday evening, at one of those
' bonnet hops' which were introduced by the officers
of the *Indus*, and which have become so popular
with the ladies. Boats were in attendance at the
Dockyard at four p.m., and by five o'clock the
greater portion of the company having assembled,
dancing commenced on the spacious main deck,
which was most tastefully decorated. Refresh-

ments were served in the ward-room, which is
beautifully fitted up. Among the guests were a
large number of French officers, who appeared to
be highly delighted with the engaging manners of
les belles Acadiennes. The fine band of the *St. George*
discoursed excellent music, and the dancing was
kept up with great spirit until ten o'clock, when
the National Anthems of France and England were
played. The officers of the *St. George* were most
assiduous in their attention to their guests. The
early part of the afternoon having been wet, the
most admirable arrangements were made in the
way of awnings, covered gangways and boats, but
fortunately, about four o'clock, the rain ceased and
the evening became beautifully fine."

On the 16th September, the French Admiral and
the officers of his squadron, gave a return ball to
the Navy and inhabitants. A more tastefully decorated ball-room I never recollect to have seen;
certainly, the French beat us fairly in decorative
art. The trophies of arms were beautifully arranged,
and the *coup d'œil*, on entering the ball-room, was
magnificent. Unlike ourselves, under similar circumstances, the French officers did everything in
their power to provide partners for their guests.

And now we come to our amateur theatricals,
which furnished amusement, not only to ourselves,
but the inhabitants of Halifax also, for some little
time.

A Mr. B——, and his wife, were the lessees of
the building, which is dignified by the name of the
"Theatre Royal, Halifax." Now it occurred to
them that an amateur performance for their benefit
would be a very profitable speculation; so they set
to work and persuaded the officers mentioned in
the following bills to undertake the parts therein
assigned to them. Did you ever undertake a part in
an amateur play? If you have not tried that way of
making yourself look foolish in public, I should recommend you not to do so. But then I speak feelingly.

Our troubles began early. The first thing was
the selection of a suitable play, and opinions differed
widely as to what would suit our company best. *That*
point settled, the next thing was to cast the piece,
and as each one wished for a creditable part, we had
considerable difficulty in filling up the subordinate
characters. *That* accomplished, our individual
work began. We copied out our respective lessons
and commenced learning them; and as every one
seemed to think that reading and spouting aloud was
the best way of committing it to memory, the conversation was for some days of a character which
would have induced a belief in the mind of an un-
initiated hearer, that we had gone mad *en masse.*

"My dear Charlotte, my beloved Charlotte!"—
"Blood and 'ouns, but she's a likely-looking filly!"
—"Help, help! Who cries for help?"—"It's no
use talking, I *will* be master in my own house!"—

THEATRE ROYAL SPRING GARDENS.

STAGE MANAGER, MR. DAVENPORT.

On WEDNESDAY Evening, September the 18th,
THE GRAND AMATEUR PERFORMANCE
BY THE OFFICERS OF
H.M.S. ST. GEORGE,
WILL TAKE PLACE, UNDER THE DISTINGUISHED PATRONAGE OF
CAPTAIN THE HON. F. EGERTON, R.N.

PREVIOUS TO THE COMEDY
AN ORIGINAL PROLOGUE
WILL BE SPOKEN BY
MR. DENNYS, R.N.

The following is the Cast of Characters for Coleman's celebrated Play
THE JEALOUS WIFE.

MR. OAKLEY	by	MR. NESHAM, R.N.
MAJOR OAKLEY	by	CAPTAIN SEARLE, R.M.L.I.
CHARLES OAKLEY	by	MR. DELME RADCLYFFE, R.N.
LORD TRINKET	by	MR. GOLDSON, R.N.
RUSSET	by	MR. DENNYS, R.N.
SIR HARRY BEAGLE	by	LIEUT. ST. JOHN, R.M.L.I.
JOHN	by	MR. FRANCIS, R.N.
PARIS	by	MR. TALBOT, R.N.
LADY FRANCIS' SERVANT	by	MR. BRUCE, R.N.
MRS. OAKLEY	by	MRS. BARROW.
LADY FRANCIS FREELOVE	by	MR. BOURKE, R.N.
HARRIET RUSSETT	by	MRS. DAVENPORT.
TOILET	by	MR. AITKINS, R.N.
CHAMBERMAID	by	MR. LUCKCRAFT, R.N.

THE FINE BAND OF THE "ST. GEORGE" WILL PERFORM DURING THE EVENING.

To conclude with the amusing Farce
P. P., OR, THE MAN AND THE TIGER.

SPLASHER	- - - -	LIEUT. VIDAL, R.N.
STARTLE	- - - -	MR. DENNYS, R.N.
LIEUT. FUSILE	- - - -	LIEUT. ALSTON, R.N.
BOB BUCKSKIN	- - - -	LIEUT. MAQUAY, R.N.
SOMERHILL	- - - -	LIEUT. HEMMANS, R.M.L.I.
SERVANT	- - - -	MR. DELME RADCLYFFE, R.N.
SUSAN STARTLE	- - - -	MRS. DAVENPORT.
CRAPE	- - - -	MRS. BARROW.
DUSTER	- - - -	MR. AITKINS, R.N.

The Plan for Seats is now Ready, at Messrs. Hall and Beamish's; where Tickets can be procured.

DUE NOTICE WILL BE GIVEN OF
MRS. BARROW'S FAREWELL BENEFIT.
Doors open at Half-past Seven.—Commence at Eight.

THEATRE ROYAL SPRING GARDENS.

STAGE MANAGER, MR. DAVENPORT.

FRIDAY Evening, September the 27th.

COMPLIMENTARY BENEFIT TO

MRS. BARROW.

Under the Distinguished Patronage of Rear-Admiral Sir Alexander
Milne, K.C.B., and Lady Milne; Maj.-Gen. Trollope, C.B.,
Commanding the Forces; Lieut.-Col. Daubeney, C.B., 62nd
Regiment; Captain the Hon. F. Egerton, H.M.S. *St. George;*
Captain Barnard, H.M.S. *Nile.*

*By kind permission of Capt. Cockburn, R.N., the splendid Band of the
"Diadem" will perform an Overture, and play during the Evening.*

GRAND UNITED SERVICE

AMATEUR PERFORMANCE

By the Officers of the Royal Artillery and Royal Engineers, by the
Officers of H.M.S. *Nile,* and the Officers of H.M.S. *St. George.*

THE ADMIRABLE PETITE COMEDY

THE DEAD SHOT.

CAPTAIN CANNON	by	MR. DYROM, R.E.
HECTOR TIMID	by	CAPT. DUMERESQ, R.A.
MR. WISEMAN	by	CAPT. CAREY, R.A.
FREDERICK THORNTON	by	MR. JONES, R.A.
WILLIAMS	by	MR. LOCOCK, R.E.
LOUISA LOVETRICK	by	MRS. BARROW.
CHATTER	by	MRS. DAVENPORT.

To be followed by that inimitable Farce, by John M. Morton,

WHITEBAIT AT GREENWICH.

MR. BENJAMIN BUZZARD	- -	DR. LLOYD, R.N.
MR. GLIMMER	- - - - -	LIEUT. SUTHER, R.M.
JOHN SMALL	- - - - -	MR. COLES, R.N.
MISS LUCRETIA BUZZARD	-	MRS. BARROW.
SALLY (a Servant)	- - - -	MRS. DAVENPORT.

AN ORIGINAL ADDRESS, WRITTEN FOR THE OCCASION,

WILL BE SPOKEN BY

MRS. BARROW

IN THE COURSE OF THE EVENING.

In conclusion Charles Mathews' mirth-provoking Farce,

TAMING THE GORILLA.

CHARLES BEESWING (Traveller in Wines) LIEUT. MAQUAY, R.N.

MR. CHILI CHAUTREE {(a Retired Ben-} MR. DENNYS, R.N.
{gal Merchant)}

JACOB MUTTER (a Servant) - - MR. DELME RADCLYFFE, R.N.

The Plan for Reserved Seats is now ready, at Messrs. Hall and
Beamish's, where tickets can be procured.

Doors open at Half-past Seven. — Commence precisely at Eight.
VIVAT REGINA.

" You false, cruel man, you!"—" Cut a caper, sing
a song, or fight you for a shilling."—" Come along,
Sir John, I know she's here;"—and so on.

Now and then a quartermaster's head might be
seen protruding for an instant into the mess, with
a message, such as " Your boat's manned, sir," to
some one of the midshipmen, who would vent his
disgust in language which might be very theatrical,
but was certainly very unparliamentary, to the
astonishment of the steady-going old petty officer.

But it was not alone the acting which taxed our
energies. We had only two ladies for a play which
required some five or six, so we had to rig out two
or three of our midshipmen in feminine attire to
support the *rôle*. But how to obtain the dresses was
a *fixer*. However, a crinoline from one, a dress from
another, and something else from a third, enabled
us to complete satisfactory costumes for two of our
representative females. One, however, there was
(Lady Freelove) whose length of leg was so great
that no dress or appendages could be found tall
enough to fit. Affairs grew desperate; at last the
manager's wife succeeded in procuring the necessary
articles, to the great joy of the company at large,
for they had each been dunning their lady acquaintances for articles of female attire of all descriptions
till they were tired of trying to find a correct fit for
her ladyship.

At length the eventful night arrived. I had

foolishly undertaken to speak the prologue, and when
the curtain drew up found myself in front of an
audience comprising the *élite* of Halifax. But to dis-
tinguish a single face was a matter of impossibility.
However, I went on, gathering courage as I proceeded, but with a momentarily increasing inability
to discover which was the floor and which the
ceiling.   It was very much the sensation one must
have in trying to walk upon a plank upside down
with suckers to the feet.   At last the abominable
address ended, and I, with feelings of immense relief,
retired behind the wings, and the play commenced,
N—— leading off.

Everything went very well till the third scene,
in which Mrs. D—— (to whom in the play I performed the part of father) had to come on ; but when
it came to the scratch no daughter made her appearance, and in spite of the most energetic telegraphing
from the manager's wife, who was on at the time,
obstinately refused to appear.   Our remonstrances
were useless.   She declared that until a little out-
standing account of dollars and cents had been
settled she would not come on the stage.   All this
while those on the boards kept saying, " Here she
comes," as required by the text of the play, but
unfortunately she *did not* come, so that there was an
obvious hitch in the proceedings which, but for the
extreme goodnature of the audience, would, no
doubt, have been noticed in the way peculiar to

theatrical assemblages when they disapprove of
aught on the stage. The manager succumbed to
circumstances and "shelled out." "My daughter"
came, and the wheels properly greased got again into
good working order.

But such a precedent was too good to be neglected. In the next act the scene-shifter refused to
change the drops, &c., unless *his* little account was
also settled in hard cash. We should have taken
matters into our own hands by main force, had we
known how to work the machinery; but the cunning
party had so fixed everything that none but him
could work it. If we attempted to touch a tricing-
line or other working part, the scene was sure to
descend in an undignified and hurried way, which
by no means contributed to the effect of the piece,
so we had to knock under, and the manager a second
time drew a cheque on the doorkeeper and paid the
refractory stage carpenter.

After this things went pretty straight, and we
finished our performance without further mis-
chance.

The following extract from the morning paper
would be very complimentary, were it not unfortunately a fact that *it was actually written six hours
before the performance took place!*

"AMATEUR PERFORMANCE AT THE THEATRE.—Last
evening a large and brilliant audience assembled to
witness a Comedy and Farce performed by the officers

of H.M.S. *St. George*, and we can safely say every one left with perfect feelings of pleasure.   The amateurs distinguished themselves; the acting was capital and elicited great applause; indeed, nothing occurred to mar the effectiveness of the representation.   Captain Searle as Major Oakley performed like an old stager, and Mr. Goldson's Lord Trinket was well conceived and executed.   Mr. Dennys spoke a very appropriate address, and also represented two old men capitally; Mr. Nesham was Mr. Oakley, and acted well up to Mrs. Barrow, who presented an admirable Mrs. Oakley.   In make-up and action Mr. Bourke as Lady Freelove was quite excellent, the undertaking was a most difficult one, and he deserves great credit for the successful effort.   Mr. D. Radclyffe made a very good Charles, and Mr. St. John was perfectly at home as Sir Harry Beagle. The servants acted by some of the Midshipmen created great merriment.   In the Farce, Mr. Vidal, Mr. Maquay, and Mr. Dennys sustained the principal parts with great effect; Mr. Hemmans also did all that was possible as Mr. Somerhill.   In short, the gentlemen may congratulate themselves that they achieved more than was probably expected, a decided success, and we in common with a large community shall be delighted to see further efforts made."

I do not know that I have ever read a notice which put on the "puff" more equally; every actor being

mentioned and praised in rotation. The critic, whoever he was, had evidently determined to do his
duty fairly by all alike, and serve out his allowance
of flattery with strict impartiality.

After the plays were over we had supper at the
" Halifax." As every one knows what sort of affair
this would-be, it is needless to particularize the number of toasts drank or songs sang; suffice it to say,
that we were jolly *ad libitum*.

On the 27th September, another amateur theatrical performance took place, the *Nile*, Garrison, and
ourselves each taking part. Ours was a failure; but
I have seldom seen better acting than that of one
or two of the officers of the *Nile* and Garrison.

On the 3rd October, another " Bonnet hop"—
or rather *Assemblage* I should call it, according to
Halifax parlance—was given by us, to which, as on
the former occasion, the youth and beauty of the
town were invited. Greatly to the disappointment
of our fair guests, the Prince did not return to the
ship until the following day; on the evening of
which, however, the majority were able to console
themselves for not having seen him on board, by
attending a ball given by the Commander-in-Chief,
at which he was present. R—— told me, on his
return, an amusing little incident connected with
this same ball.

It appears that during one of those awkward
pauses in conversation which will occasionally occur

even when dancing with the most lively partners ····
one of those moments, in fact, when the gentleman
is mentally saying to himself, "What *can* I talk
about? what a muff she must think me!"—that
R——, by way of saying something, began talking
about the recent amateur theatricals. The lady was
quite unaware that her gallant partner had been one
of the actors whose powers he was criticizing,
and naively remarked to him, "Well, Mr. D——
acted pretty well, and so did Mr. M——, *but that
abominable servant, Jacob, spoilt everything!*" R——
was rather taken aback, but after a few minutes, told
her that he was the identical *Jacob* referred to, upon
which, with commendable firmness, she replied—
"Well, I'm not going to tell you you acted well,
even if you *are* the party in question."

M—— (who had just arrived in the *Rinaldo* from
New York) came on board one evening, and amused
us much by his yarns about the Yankees. Amongst
others he told us the following :—

In the *New York Times* (or some other leading
paper) this laconic notice was inserted. The italics
are my own.

"An individual was found last night lying in
Sixth Avenue-street, with his jaw broken and one
eye completely gouged out. *There is a suspicion of
foul play*" ! ! ! —(I should rather imagine there
was.)

I subjoin the following account, taken from the

daily papers, of a review which took place on the 13th October:—

" NAVAL REVIEW.—The crews, including marines, of H.M.S. *Nile, St. George, Diadem,* and *Immortalité,* marched from the Dockyard yesterday morning to the common, where a grand field-day took place. The view from the Citadel of the evolutions of the quickly moving masses, and the continuous firing of the heavy field-pieces and small arms, was not only a very beautiful and animated spectacle, but produced in the mind a vivid realization of actual warfare.

" The marines and marine artillery fired several volleys, by companies and in line, but they seemed for the most part to be kept as a reserve—the sailors taking the initiative in the battle, and, as their appearance would certainly indicate, put the ' enemy' to flight without the assistance of their soldier shipmates. It is a matter of surprise how Jack Tars could have been moulded into such good soldiers. The firing of the marines was equal to any we have ever seen on the Common—some of the companies fired as one man.

The crews arrived at the Common about nine o'clock, and finished their exercises about half-past eleven o'clock. They were then drawn in line, and marched through several streets of the city. After reaching the South End they proceeded through Hollis, Granville, and Water streets to the Dockyard, in the following order:—Band of *Nile*, marine artillery, marines, heavy field-pieces drawn by sailors, officers and seamen of *Nile;* band of *Diadem*, officers and seamen of *Diadem* and *Immortalité;* band of *St. George*, officers and seamen of *St. George.* In the ranks of the latter we noticed Prince Alfred, who had of course taken his part in the fatigues of the day, in his capacity as midshipman.

" This spectacle, comprising but a small portion of the British navy, with a son of Queen Victoria occupying a subordinate position in the ranks, might well impress the beholder with an idea of the power of our parent nation, and with a belief in the Nelsonic motto, that ' England expects every man to do his duty.'

" This was probably the largest turn out of sailors and marines that has ever been seen in the streets of Halifax—marching in fours, they made a line extending over the largest part of Upper Water-street. Large numbers of persons gathered on the side-walks to witness the passing of this formidable body of men.

" We regret to learn that one or two accidents occurred to seamen working the large guns; we have not, however, been able to ascertain to what extent they were injured."

One of our officers possessed a large dog of the Newfoundland species. After the review it was found that he had been shot in three places, and was therefore, as a matter of humanity, killed. Were it possible to detect the parties who thus wantonly fired at the poor *dog*, they would form, I imagine, fit objects for the application of the *cat*.

The foliage of the trees was just beginning to change into those beautiful " autumn tints," which nowhere are to be seen in greater perfection than here. Every tint, from crimson to russet-brown, seemed to be visible in the trees. So beautiful are many of the leaves that the ladies of Halifax make collections of them; they are gummed on sheets of card-board and then varnished, and will, it is said, by this treatment retain their colour for a considerable time.

Amongst the curiosities of the neighbourhood may be mentioned the slip for conveying the wood floated down to the end of the Windsor Canal into the sea, on boats, and from the sea into the canal. It would be almost impossible, without a diagram, to give an idea of this ingenious arrangement; it is worth a visit from any of my readers who may visit Halifax.

M

CHAPTER XI.

AMONGST the amusements at Halifax cricket was, as
might be expected, a favourite one with the officers
of both services.   Several matches were played between the Garrison and the Navy, the eleven of the
latter being chosen from the *Nile* and *St. George.*
The ground is situated about a mile from the town,
and the drive to and from it, in 'busses hired for the
occasion, was a source of great amusement to the
juniors of both messes, and a time of mortal terror
to the nervous party who was the legitimate driver.
Amateur Jehus abounded among us, but few handled
the ribbons better than my friend T——, who was
accordingly considered honorary 'bus driver to the
Club, an arrangement which did not, I am afraid,
add to the comfort of the unlucky horses.

, The Garrison Club was composed of the 63rd
and part of the 62nd Regiment, and some of the
Artillery and Engineers.   They had a very good
eleven, but were occasionally beaten by the Navy.
One great advantage attendant on this game was the
fact, that whereas in most ports naval officers have

but a formal acquaintance with those of the sister service, the constantly meeting each other in the cricket field, either as players or lookers-on, produced a very intimate and friendly feeling between the army and navy at Halifax.

First and foremost among the sports of Nova Scotia comes fishing. I cannot say that I know much about it myself, being of opinion that, in my case at least, Dr. Johnson's definition of a fishing-rod "being a stick with a fool at one end and a worm at the other" is strictly correct. I never could (shade of Izaak Walton forgive me!) find the slightest satisfaction in "flogging the water" for four or five hours at a stretch, rewarded perhaps by a couple of fish which were not worth the trouble of dressing. But though thus lamentably deficient myself in sporting zeal, I happen to have heard a good deal about sporting matters while at Halifax, and will record my knowledge, such as it is, for the benefit of any reader who may take an interest in such matters.

Allow me then to introduce to you Mr. Fredericks, whose card I insert hereunder:—

CHARLES FREDERICKS,

THE NOVA SCOTIA FISHERMAN,

Who during the Fishing Season lives on the Banks of the Rivers and Lakes of the Province.

A more enthusiastic angler I have seldom met.
Both in theory and practice he is without an equal in
the province; and the attention he bestows on those
who consult him is extreme. Would you know
the most killing flies, the best streams, or the most
advisable outfit on proceeding on a fishing excursion,
he is the best authority from whom to seek advice.
Many of our officers (F—— and C—— especially)
were extremely fond of this pastime, and thanks to
Mr. Fredericks' courtesy, were often enabled to make
a good day's sport, when less fortunate anglers were
obliged to return with tenantless creels.

The most favourite stream seemed to be the
Shubernacketie River. "Still Waters," "Spider
Lake," and the lakes beyond the north-west arm,
each had their admirers also. Fishing streams or
lakes are not preserved in Nova Scotia, so that one
can enjoy a day's sport in any part of the country
without the oft-times troublesome formality of
obtaining permission from the tenant or owner of
the lands in which the water may be situated.

The finest salmon fishing is, without doubt, to be
got at Margaree, which is on the western side of the
peninsula. Salmon of fabulous weight are reported
to have yielded to the persuasive temptations held
out (from the end of a stout rod) by skilled
amateurs; and were the place a little more accessible
it would, I have no doubt, be crowded by lovers of
the sport. As it is, it is but seldom visited, save by

residents in the colony, as at least five or six days'
leave must be obtained to start from Halifax with
any hope of a tolerable stay.

Sea trout abound in the Nova Scotian waters.
As for deep-sea fishing, they enjoy so world wide a
reputation in that respect, that it is needless for me
to discuss the question here.

Next to fishing comes shooting ; not that which
is understood by this term in England, in the way of
game, but bear and moose hunting.   The former is
a tolerably dangerous sport, as even Nova Scotia
bears are sometimes vicious, especially after the
receipt in their stomachs of a charge of large shot,
in which case, if unprovided with a second edition,
retreat is advisable when possible. But moose hunting
is, to say the best of it, a rather mild amusement,
the only excitement being in the attempt to get
sufficiently near the animal, off the wind, to bring
him well within range.   Although nature has provided these animals with a most powerful aggressive
weapon, in the shape of antlers, they seldom attempt
to use them, preferring flight to fighting. Of course
now and then they turn at bay ; but, generally
speaking, one need not feel under particular appre-
hension for the safety of any friends who may have
gone out on an expedition to kill moose.

Moose have been seen and killed near the shores
of the basin which forms the upper end of the harbour, though their presence so close to the town is

of rare occurrence.   Bears too have been found in
the grounds of a gentleman living but three miles
from Dartmouth.   The usual hunting ground is,
however, from thirty to forty miles in the interior.

If you follow the main road to the Mills, at the
extremity of the north-west arm of the harbour, till
you reach a small wooden bridge, and then turn off
sharply to the right, you will come to the house·
and grounds of a Mr. Downs, who possesses a very
nice little collection of animals and birds, living and
stuffed.   He is a capital taxidermist, and his stuffed
moose heads have once or twice carried off the prize
at local exhibitions.

The country round Halifax is thickly overgrown
with wood.   Huge boulders of rock cover every
foot of ground between the trees ; so thickly do they
lie, that it is estimated to cost 200*l.* per acre to clear
it.   Whence they come is a mystery. Nothing but
a previous universal submergence ·of Nova Scotia
explains their appearance satisfactorily to my mind ;
but knowing but little of geology, I leave to wiser
heads than mine the discussion of this question.
Certain it is, that there they are, and that most of
the colonists prefer cultivating the shallow depth of
earth around and above them to the herculean task
of clearing them away and thoroughly ploughing
the soil.

Wild fruits, such as strawberries and raspberries,
abound in the hedges and underwood. As for berries

of other kinds, their names and colours are legion. The blue berry is the most common, and a piece of grass plat thickly studded with them presents a most brilliant appearance, the berry being of a most beautiful violet colour. Most English fruits are obtainable in Nova Scotia. Bermuda supplies, however, the greater part of the potatoes and yams consumed.

As for Halifax itself, the town presents a curious appearance to any one fresh from England ; nearly all the houses being built of wood, or at least those lining the waterside. The churches rising upwards here and there, being, for the most part, of the same material, painted white, spires included, look like models constructed of cardboard. Of course such buildings are highly inflammable, and fires are of nightly occurrence. They have a well-organized fire brigade which is always ready at a moment's notice, but, unfortunately, seems generally to suffer from a want of water when its services are most needed, and thus wastes a vast amount of zeal to no purpose. It is a favourite " lark " with fast young men to raise a cry of fire in the streets, and as the bells of every church in the neighbourhood are set ringing on such an alarm, and the inhabitants rush about in a state of terror and nudity, which do not contribute by any means to the aid of the brigade, a pretty good commotion may be easily caused in this manner.

As for the society of Halifax, we certainly cannot complain of any want of hospitality amongst those whose acquaintance we made. With respect to the town generally, the magnificent return made by it for our balls and "bonnet hops" will ever leave a lasting impression on the minds of the officers of the *St. George*.

It is astonishing how many naval and military officers get caught in the matrimonial noose at Halifax. But allow me to give one warning— *They are all cousins;* so beware what you say, or rather, to quote the old proverb,

> "*Of* whom you speak, *to* whom you speak,
> And *how*, and *when*, and *where*."

Many were the picnics in which we joined during the summer months; the day's fun being generally wound up by a dance at the house of one or other of our friends.

A very amusing petition was presented to the Provincial Parliament a short time before our arrival, of which I give a copy below. It is a *bonâ fide* document, but was, I suppose, the production of some wag whom the petitioner had requested to write it out for him. Anyhow, it caused an immense deal of laughter amongst the governing powers. Whether the *Captain* got his petition granted, I do not know; but he certainly made out a strong case.

" To dem honorble Gemblmns dat libs in dat dar big, brown house way down to Halifax.

" De humble petition of Juba, ex-Captain ob de *Shubblenose*, and Commr.-in-Chief ob all de cullad individuals in and about de village of Hansport,

" Humbly Shewiff,—Dat wereas in de munth of July las, de Honbl. Capn. Vesey, of H.M.B. ship *Styx*, did requess of dis Honbl. Capn. Juba (dat's me myself, dat is), ob de *Shubblenose*, dat he (*me*) would anchor, or cause to be anchored, dis said *Shubblenose* at de deepest part ob de channel, dat she might searb as a (black) buoy to shew de Honbl. Cap. Vesey whar he might drop his mudhood safe.

"An' whereas de Hon. Capn. Juba (dat's me agin) acted 'cordin' to 'quess ob de brodder ossifer, an' did anchor dis de *Shubblenose* at dat dar spessified diggins ; and wharas de *Styx* did come wid his assistance safely, but in so doing, did run fowl of youah perditioner's vessel, an' smash an' mash her all to smidderee.

" Darefore dis darkey, youah perditioner, am ob de undewided opinion dat as de wassel war lost in de Gubberment service, darefore dis Gubberment orter pay for de same, darefore he humbly requesses ob youah honorble gemblmn dat you will be pleesed to grant dis niggah a sum of twenty dollars ! as a small damnification for de loss sustained by dis African gemblmn, de Honble. Capn. Juba, &c. &c.

(dat's me), else he swar his life agin you sartin.
Youah perditioner had some idea ob demandin'
damages ob de Home Gubberment : but in 2nd
toughts, for fear such a course might involve Great
Brittain in a war wid dis country, he concluded to
luff it drop, hopin' dat youah honble. body will do
de agreeble, and youah perditioner, as in duty bound,
will eber sing."

There is one street of the town which is exclusively inhabited by darkies, and is, as might be
expected, the dirtiest in Halifax. The black women
gain their living chiefly by selling berries, &c. when
in season.

The American element largely prevails here.
You order American editions of books, and in fact
American everythings, from patent corkscrews to
patent baby jumpers. One thing which is American
allow me, in the strongest terms, to recommend,
viz. preserved milk. I have forgotten the name on
the tin, but the factory is, I know, situate in Mas-
sachusetts. Any one who has made a voyage of a
few hundred miles will quite appreciate the comfort
of having a good substitute for milk ; so all I can
say to intending voyagers is, lay in a stock betimes.

One sport essentially Haligonian I have forgotten
to mention. Dear me, what could I have been about
to talk about fishing, and not take any notice of
lobsters ? for lobster spearing is the sport in ques-

tion. Ladies and gentlemen alike indulge in this
amusement; but when I speak of lobster *spearing*,
do not imagine for one moment that a sharp-pointed
steel weapon is the instrument of capture. Fancy
a lady leaning over the gunwale of a boat watching
her intended victim crawling comfortably along the
bottom, and then transfixing it with a *scraunch*, such
as is produced by driving a pair of scissor points
through the defensive armour of a cray fish. Such
a pastime would hardly find favour with the fair sex.
No, the ways to catch lobsters in Halifax harbour
are (putting aside baskets or nets) two : the one
being to tuck your trousers up, and wade in bare-
footed till an excruciating grip of the big toe informs
you that you have caught your lobster, or rather
that he has caught you ; the other (which I prefer)
being to provide yourself with a long-forked pole,
which, when pressed down hard over the back of
the fish, holds him in its embrace till you can draw
him from the water and safely deposit him in the
bottom of the boat. By the bye, they say snakes
are sometimes caught in this manner ; but to do
this to a reptile seems to me very much like putting
salt on a bird's tail to catch him, as it requires, in
the first place, a closer proximity than either parties
are likely to wish for if it can possibly be helped.

The number of lobsters caught in this way is
enormous. Some individual, evidently of a statis-
tical turn of mind, computed, I believe, that some

two and a half millions was the annual average.
Truly, they abound everywhere in Halifax; and
they became a favourite diet in our mess, their
shells forming handy missiles, and their cost being
small.

And now we quit Halifax, though not for good.
Should this ever meet the eye of former friends in
that neighbourhood, may they take my remarks in
good part, and be sure that many pleasant memories
are connected in the minds of the *St. George's* with
their visit to the capital of Nova Scotia.

CHAPTER XII.

NOVA SCOTIA GOLDFIELDS.—SYDNEY.

On the 18th October, the *St. George* left Halifax
(having on board Lord Mulgrave, the Governor of
the colony, and other gentlemen), accompanied by
the *Nimble*, carrying the flag (temporarily) of Vice-
Admiral Sir Alexander Milne, the Commander-in-
Chief. We arrived at Ship Harbour (which is but
from thirty to forty miles to the northward of
Halifax), about one p.m. the same day.

The following morning, Prince Alfred accompanied the Captain and Major Cowell to the *Nimble*,
and all officers who wished to go up to the Tangier
gold-diggings, found their way on board her also.
She steamed up about seven miles (if measured in a
straight line), and anchored off the town of Tangier,
and in a short time we had all disembarked in as
unsoiled a manner as the landing-place would
permit.

The first appearance of both diggers and houses
was not cheering : I really do not know which pre-

sented the worse appearance. The style of edifice
was varied according to the taste of the owner,
though, certainly, a wooden shanty does not afford
much scope to architectural genius. The most aris-
tocratic looking were constructed of planed boards;
less aspiring householders being content with the
rough log,—with shingles for the roofing material
in both cases.

The habitations might, perhaps, be called houses
by a slight stretch of courtesy; but the roads—no,
not roads, but apologies for them—were certainly
not to be called by any term which indicates a
passable highway. The mud (where it was not a
pond) was about eleven inches in depth, at least.
An immense quantity of fir branches had been cut
down to serve as a sort of temporary macadamiza-
tion; the result being that one walked on a spongy
compound of greenstuff and soft mud, to the great
detriment of one's personal appearance about the
boots and legs. Personal appearance, however, in
this part of the world, was, fortunately, but a
secondary consideration; most of those who were
enthusiastically welcoming His Royal Highness
being in a costume which was hardly suited for the
polite localities of Oxford or Regent-street. Very
varied and picturesque was the appearance of many
of the crowd. Long hair and beards, fur caps, red
flannel shirts, and great *he-boots*, composed a *tout
ensemble* which well accorded with one's idea of the

gambusino so well described in "Con Cregan," but which would tend (especially with the accompaniments of bowie knife and revolver) to make a timid man nervous, if forced into too close companionship with them with valuables in his possession. Yet underneath this ferocious guise many a civil spoken person there was, who might have been recognised by an old acquaintance, as some erst smooth-shaven friend, whose daily avocation at desk or counter had been for a time abandoned to dig for gold. I must say, that their welcome to the Prince was as warm as circumstances would admit of, and their civility to ourselves great.

The Prince and party were first of all taken to see the most successful pits, and the machinery, such as it was, employed in the process of gold seeking; but some four or five of us preferred, first of all, taking a pipe in a most inviting-looking little dell; and then cruising about by ourselves, to use our eyes and ears without the assistance of a cicerone.

The first place we visited (having finished our pipes) was a shaft situated on a small hill to the left of the road. Four Americans were the owners thereof, and they answered all our questions in the fullest manner. After talking a few minutes, we were requested to step back a little, as two blasts were about to be fired, and the pieces of rock were given to flying about in eccentric directions. We asked if they could strike us where we were standing.

"Wa'al, perhaps.   By Jehosaphat, I guess there's blood drawn already," exclaimed our interlocutor, pointing to a man who was rushing about at the bottom of the rise with a red-hot iron in his hand, with which he had just fired the "blast," and who had been struck on the hand, which was bleeding, by a piece of rock.

As he spoke there was a whir-r-r of stones flying past us, and a report, as if a musket had been fired. We had expected the noise to be very much greater, but were perfectly satisfied that the stones had been near enough to be pleasant.   So we guessed we'd "vamos."

We visited, in company with the person we had first addressed, several pits.   The precious metal is not found distributed over any wide extent of quartz.   On the contrary, the quartz veins in no place exceeded some four or five inches in width, the surrounding material being slate.   Gold digging out here must be no joke, for the quartz is hard as adamant, and the picks and bars used in breaking it out require constant hardening and sharpening. The deepest pit at the Tangier diggings is about forty feet in depth ; in other gold producing coun-tries, pits of from 300 to 400 feet are frequently met with.   Those with whom we conversed, stated that it was believed that productive veins would be found here at that distance below the surface; but that no private individuals possessed either means or money to dig on speculation a well such as a pit of this depth would be. They added, that were the *find* to become a little more profitable, they had no doubt that a company would be formed for the purpose.

The nearest approach to mining on a large scale is a tunnel commenced on the side of a hill, which is said to consist mainly of auriferous quartz; the results obtained from it as yet, however, had been small, but strong hopes were entertained of eventually reaching some very rich veins.

Our American friend insisted on our coming up to his hut, and taking a drop of refreshment before returning to the ship. He handed us a pannikin containing a liquor which he called *coffee*. Had I seen the wink with which he accompanied his speech, I should have hesitated before taking a draught such as I did; for the said coffee was fiery rum, stronger than I ever remember to have tasted before, so that my breath was for the time completely taken out of me.

When I had recovered wind, and our host had done laughing at the "sell," he explained to us how the gold was extracted from the ore—how quicksilver was used in the operation, and many other details which, though they interested me at

N

the time, would I fear only, if described, tire the
patience of my readers.

We then bid good day to our obliging acquaintance, and returned to the landing-place; but
before going off, entered a shed close by to see a
steam-crushing machine, which consisted of a heavy
iron wheel of about eight feet in diameter and about
twenty inches in width at its outer edge.   This
was kept continually revolving in a circular pan of
cast iron, and the bits of quartz were successively
brought under its heavy rim; having been sufficiently crushed, they were carried by a small stream
of water into a washing trough, and thence into
various shallower ones, during its progress through
which the precious metal was separated from the
ground rock.   I should add, that the quartz is
previously submitted to the action of fire, to render
it more easily broken.

A water-power crushing machine was in course
of erection on the bank of a small stream which
runs through the settlement.   On making inquiry
about it from our Yankee friend before alluded to,
whom we again met, he informed us that it was a
joint speculation between a farmer, a blacksmith,
and a millwright.   " But I guess," continued he,
" that it'll be a failure.   They haven't no *science*,
sir-ree; poor deluded critters, to think that they
could build a crusher with not an ounce of science
in their brains between them.   Jehosaphat! but it

riles me." I did not quite see the force of his remark, being of opinion that mechanical skill was
the chief requisite, and ventured to insinuate as
much.

"And do you think *I* would come and look for
gold if I hadn't a tip-top scientific knowledge," re-
sponded the indignant American. "Brains ain't
nothing, I guess, without science; no, sir-ree."

So we left him still indignant at our disrespect
for science.

There was a very good story told of the authorities here, for the truth of which, however, I cannot
vouch; but, such as I heard it, here it is.

It appears that, anxious to please the Prince, they
had caused a nugget to be buried in a certain spot
which it was intended that he should himself dig
over, and so disinter the precious lump. It was,
as they imagined, buried under all requisite precau-
tions to ensure secrecy, it being consigned to the
ground at night when the neighbourhood was clear;
but they reckoned without their host, for a juvenile
of lax moral principles was prowling about near the
place and witnessed the, to him, strange proceeding
of digging up and replacing a few shovelfuls of
earth with no apparent object in view. Waiting
till the parties employed had taken their departure,
he proceeded to satisfy his curiosity by imitating
their example, and after scratching up the earth for
a slight depth, was rewarded by finding the nugget,

which he carried off in triumph. Next day the
intended owner, viz., His Royal Highness, went
through the same ceremony, as far as the digging
was concerned, but with a less satisfactory result to
the authorities and himself. The unfortunate little
scamp, however, had been by this time detected,
having, I suppose, imprudently shown his prize or
made mention of it to some one; so he received
summary punishment by flagellation on a sensitive
part of his body, which, I trust, taught him two
useful lessons—not to be too curious, and not to
appropriate what was very clearly not his own, even
supposing it to be unclaimed by any one else.

A controversy on the capabilities of the goldfields was raging in the papers when we quitted
Halifax. One party asserting that an over-coloured •
picture was drawn of them to tempt people to take
lots. The others as vehemently declaiming against
the selfishness of those who would keep the labourer
and artisan from the chance of acquiring independence, which the mines presented. For my own
part, I should say, from the opportunity I had of
seeing Tangier, and conversing with many who
were thoroughly acquainted with the country, that
one might earn good workman's wages by gold
digging, but little more. Very few cases had occurred of men becoming suddenly wealthy from luck
in this way. Very hard work and constant expo-
sure seem necessary elements of a digger's life in

Nova Scotia, and I would certainly not advise any one to emigrate to that country at present to try their fortune with the pick and cradle.

Many specimens of quartz were offered for sale, with a small portion of the precious metal peeping slyly out of a crack or hole, in just such a way as to tempt one to speculate, on the chance that the rock might contain gold throughout. Some of our officers invested, but did not, I fear, get their money's worth for their bargains.

We left Ship Harbour on the 21st October, 1861, and arrived for the second time at Sydney, Cape Breton, at four, p.m., on the 22nd.

The Prince landed the following day, and was received with the same welcome as at other places. M. B——, the French Consul, undertook to drive His Royal Highness and Major Cowell round the town to show them the *lions* of Sydney:—very tame lions, too, I am afraid. As his skill as a Jehu was not of the very first order, he may congratulate himself on having so successfully performed a duty which, in the character of a representative of our gallant allies, was no doubt extremely pleasing to him.

Any one who will take the trouble to consult a map of Nova Scotia, will perceive that it is nearly divided into two parts by a chain of lakes, one of which is called the Great Bras d'Or. In it is situated Christmas Island, whither resort yearly all the

Indians of the neighbourhood to hold a kind of fair,
carnival, and religious meeting combined.   This
usually takes place in the month of October, and all
marriages and christenings for the past year are performed on this occasion, it being impossible at all
times to secure the presence of a priest to perform
these ceremonies in the distant interior, which is
the home of many of the tribes.

The Queen of the Mic-macs is an old woman of
some sixty summers, who possesses great influence
over her tribe.   She is chiefly famous for the excellency of her porcupine quill work, which commands
a high price and ready sale in the neighbourhood,
large quantities being sent southward.   Mrs. D——
told me that some few years ago she saw a wampum
belt which was peculiarly valued by the tribe, as
the hieroglyphics worked on it recorded some events
in the dim past of tradition, the memory of which
has now passed away.   It was lost, or stolen it is
supposed, some ten years since.

I can add few remarks to my former ones about
Sydney.   We received on this occasion the same
hospitable welcome which we had previously enjoyed, and were as sorry to leave as on the former
occasion.

On the 24th of October we steamed over to North
Sydney, where the coal mines are situated for which
Nova Scotia is most famous; detained there by con-
trary winds, we did not leave that anchorage till

the following day, when we steamed out and shaped course for Louisburg.

As we were entering that harbour, about fifteen minutes to three o'clock, a man fell overboard, but fortunately contrived to reach the life-buoy, to which he clung until picked up by the cutter—almost the first time that I have seen the old-fashioned buoy prove to be of any use.

The entries in my journal for the next three days are uninteresting. We arrived at Arichat about three o'clock, p.m., on the 26th, and were obliged to remain there till the 30th, in consequence of its coming on to blow a gale of wind. The second anchor was let go, and the sheet cable cleared away, but was fortunately not needed.

We returned to Halifax on the 31st of October, 1862, and finally left that part of the station on the 19th of November.

The only circumstance of interest which occurred during this period was one, an account of which I give *in extenso* from the daily morning paper. As it is scarcely to be expected that other than freemasons will take much interest therein, I should advise those who are *not* such to skip it; while those who *are* Brethren of the Craft will learn with lively satisfaction the kindly feeling existing between the Halifax lodges and the Brethren of the *St. George.*

"MASONIC PRESENTATION.—A very interesting

meeting of the Virgin Lodge, No. 558, R. E., was held on Friday evening last at Masonic Hall, for the purpose of presenting a Mark Jewel to the Rev. William Lake Onslow, the Chaplain of H.M.S. *St. George.*

"The attendance was large to witness this pleasing ceremony, and included quite a number of officers from the various men-of-war in port as well as many Brethren from the country.

"We publish below both the address from the Lodge and the reverend gentleman's very touching reply, which was delivered with great feeling.

"We regret the public have not had an opportunity of seeing this very beautiful jewel, which was designed and executed by Mr. Cornelius. It was found necessary to present it sooner than intended, owing to a rumour of the *St. George's* early departure.

"Such occasions as these tend to cement feelings of mutual esteem between our community and strangers who may come among them, and are worthy of imitation."—*Sun.*

"*Address to the Rev. Brother Onslow, of H.M.S.
St. George.*

" REVEREND SIR AND BROTHER,

"The occasion of your early departure from our shores has impressed the minds of the members of this Lodge, who, during your sojourn amongst them,

have received so much pleasure from their association with yourself and the Brethren of the *St. George*,
as presenting a fitting opportunity to offer you some
slight token of their regard.

" From the time of your first introduction among
us by our Right Worshipful Grand Master, soon
after the arrival of the noble ship to which you are
attached, in so eminent a capacity as the Naval
instructor of one of the sons of our beloved Queen,
your zealous attendance and active co-operation
with us has been a matter of high appreciation by
every member of the Virgin Lodge.

" We cannot but remember that the illustrious
Grandsire of your Royal charge, when formerly
residing here, in the performance of some of the
most important functions of the Crown, laid with
Masonic honours the corner stone of the building
in which we are now assembled.

" It is also a pleasing incident for us to know that
one of the fairest townships of our Province bears
the honoured name of your family, many of whose
members have filled high offices of the State, and was
originally settled by one of your ancestors ; so that
in addition to the ties of our Brotherhood, we can
almost look upon you as a countryman. Nor are
we so entirely bound up in our regard for your exer-
tions in the interest of our Order as to be unable to
appreciate also your zealous discharge of the sacred
duties of your profession in our community at large,

the benefits of which will be held in grateful remembrance of many of our fellow-citizens.

"It gives us, then, the greatest pleasure to congratulate you as an honorary member of the Virgin Lodge, and to present you with a Mark Jewel, composed of Nova Scotia gold, and executed by one of our members, now handed to you by our Senior Past Master, The Honourable Alexander Keith.

"We trust that your intercourse, and that of the Brethren of your ship, with the Craft at all of the stations where you may meet them, will be as gratifying and pleasant as ours has been with you, and that, though never unprepared to confront the Dragon of War, the Red Cross may still float in peaceful folds from the *St. George*, and the hearthstones of her officers and crew made glad in due time by their happy return, with numbers undiminished by carnage or disease.

> "W. S. Symonds, Master,
> "W. A. Hesson, P.M., } Committee.
> "William Twining, P.M.,

"On behalf of Virgin Lodge."

"After which, the R.W. the Hon. Alex. Keith, Provincial Grand Master and Senior Past Master of the Virgin Lodge, invested the Reverend Brother with the Jewel, accompanying the same with a suitable address.

" *To the Right Worshipful the Grand Master of the*
Nova Scotia Lodges, the Worshipful Master of the
Virgin Lodge and its Brethren.

" RIGHT WORSHIPFUL SIR, WORSHIPFUL SIR AND
BRETHREN,—It is with great and heartfelt emotion
that I have just heard your touching and most
beautiful address.   First of all in the great compliment of making me an Honorary Member of the
Virgin Lodge, and then announcing the fact of
presenting me with a further token of that regard
and affection which binds us together in the great
Brotherhood of the Craft.

" It is indeed, at all times, most pleasing to find
that any duty or co-operation, done for the love and
sake of our Order, is appreciated, slight as it may
have been ; but how much more in my individual
case, to see how handsomely and nobly the members of the Virgin Lodge have regarded their
Brother and his humble service.

" Your allusions to my association with yourselves as nearly a countryman are most pleasing
and agreeable to me, because I must feel *its reality*
now.   For it is with no little pride that my family
name stands among the most beautiful of the townships of Nova Scotia, and especially, also, as the
founder of the same township, my ancestor, left his
large estates in Carolina, and came up to this

country for the sake of showing his attachment,
loyalty, and fidelity to the same throne and realm
over which our most gracious and beloved Queen
now reigns in the hearts of her people. I shall look
then on this Mark Jewel with great regard and
value, not only from the memory of *this scene* and
its deep interest to myself,—but that *now*, as a
countryman and Brother, I see in its pure and
beautiful gold the realization of those watchwords,

' Advance, Nova Scotia.'

" I pass on to your most kindly mention of my
labours in my own especial calling, during the
sojourn of the *St. George* in these waters, and am
indeed thankful that any work done in the name of
the Great and Almighty Ruler of our Order may
have left not only to ourselves but to others of our
fellow-citizens an impress which may not pass away
with change or time.

" The Brethren of the *St. George* and myself *cannot, will not easily* forget their relationship with
the Virgin Lodge, and in all their wide wanderings
on the ocean must remember that it is here that
so many recollections will arise which will bring
back to mind our duty and love for one another,
as Brethren of an Order which expands itself far
and wide to the extreme ends of the world, and
not the less shall we forget our obligations and
obedience to Him, the Great Architect of Creation,

whose all-seeing Eye takes in our every moral action, thoughts, words, and deeds, and who in all our meetings we invoke to bless the work and be with us.

"We thank you most heartily for those eloquent and earnest wishes, in which you bid us godspeed to our homes and hearths, and that the red cross of *St. George* may float quietly from the masthead, and although prepared for war, its horrors and dangers, may it be to us and all nations the sign of peace.

"Finally, Most Worshipful Sir, Worshipful Sir and Brethren, may we all meet in the Grand Lodge above, where all sorrow, trials, and earthly labours are at rest, and God is all and in all, and where eternal love, unity, and concord dwell with the Brethren for ever.

"WM. LAKE ONSLOW,

"Union Lodge, Malta, No. 588,

"Chaplain and Naval Instructor H.M.S. *St. George.*"

CHAPTER XIII.

ON the 19th November, 1861, we bid a final adieu to the shore of Nova Scotia, being under orders to proceed to Nassau in the Bahamas, and thence, if time permitted, to Bermuda; the latter place not to be visited unless it was found that we could reach it by the 17th of the ensuing month.

H.M. ships *Nile, Diadem,* and *Nimble* accompanied the *St. George* out of Halifax harbour, each bound for a different destination. As we steamed past the crowded piers and wharves, the people loudly cheered each ship in succession, and from the top windows of some of the higher buildings handkerchiefs might here and there be seen waving their owners' adieux to those who were now leaving them, to no doubt sincerely deplore the loss of the familiar naval uniforms whose presence had so often enlivened their pic-nics and parties.

The vessels parted company from each other in a very short time after clearing the port, the *Nile*

being bound to Bermuda, and the *Diadem* and
Nimble to the neighbourhood of Cape Sable.

On the 20th, we began to experience the effects
of a heavy swell from the north-eastward. Everything, as is usual under such circumstances, began
to fly about in the most unsatisfactory manner.
We shipped several seas in at the main deck ports,
and to make matters worse it rained heavily; so
that, between the two, the lower deck and orlop
were soon afloat. I have before noticed the peculiarly large share which always fell to the gun-room
when water was the subject, and this day's experience
formed no exception to the rule. Our cushions,
&c. &c. were soaked through in a very few minutes;
and as the ports were of necessity barred in, the
steam arising from the wet articles in the close and
hot gun-room was overpowering. Our chests again
began their acrobatic feats, as on the former occasion,
and the same discomfort reigned supreme in that
retiring room for junior naval officers, the after
cockpit.

It so happened that there were in our mess-room
two chocks of wood, which were used for running
out hawsers from the stern ports, and these chocks
(which weighed about five hundredweight each)
were lashed underneath the table. During one of
the heavy lurches which the ship was constantly
making, one of these highly useful but very unor-
namental pieces of mess furniture broke adrift from

its lashings, and the deck being very slippery from
the water, began careering backwards and forwards
from side to side of the gun-room with every roll of
the ship.   As we had but little room for stowage
below, several casks of flour, onions, potatoes, and
bottled sherry had been secured to the ship's side
till the store-room should be sufficiently clear to
admit of their being placed therein.   The very first
thing which the chock, whose liveliness was remarkable, came foul of, was the flour, and the consequences may be imagined ; the contents of the
cask mingling with the water, and forming an
impromptu dough.   Vain were our efforts to catch
the truant chock ; and vain, also, were the attempts
to muzzle it, made by a party of marines, which
had been sent below for that especial purpose ; for,
like a mad bull in a china shop, no one seemed disposed to get right in its way, as the chances of
getting one's legs broken were considerable, and
one's footing in the gun-room, at the best of times,
in such a gale of wind, is always, to say the least
of it, precarious.   After every attempt to catch it,
the chock would rush from one side to the other,
committing fresh damage with every roll.   Smash
went a cask of potatoes, which swelled the " Douglas
larder" forming in the scuppers.   Crash went a cask
of bottled sherry on the opposite side, distributing
a quantity of broken glass over the deck, thereby
materially abating the zeal of the chock-catchers,

whose bare feet were unprotected from unpleasant articles of this description. And so it went on; onions and potatoes, flour and bottled sherry, biscuit and salt water, combining to make as queer a mixture as can well be imagined.

But our five hundredweight friend had another piece of mischief to commit before he was finally secured. Some four or five in the mess had taken refuge from the rush on the top of the table, and were congratulating themselves on their safe position, when, bang! down came the whole table, midshipmen and all, to the deck, so that the table-cloths and officers formed two other elements of the above-mentioned delightful mixture. Such a scene as our mess presented at this moment, I never before saw in H.M. Service; and, to tell the truth, have no particular wish to see again.

After having done about thirty pounds' worth of damage, the chock was secured by swabs being placed round it, and was then lashed in its proper position.

During the 21st November we had just the same weather as on the previous day. The watch below were piped to turn into their hammocks, so everybody who could manage it did "beam-end exercise" instead of knocking about the decks or gun-room.

Our dinners during the time this agreeable weather lasted were certainly not à la Soyer. A large iron kettle suspended in amidships of the

o

berth did duty for trough ; and the hungry members
of our mess, each arming himself with a table-
spoon, commenced ladling the hot compound of
hash, soup, &c. into soup plates, which had to be
carefully balanced to prevent the loss of their contents—no easy matter on the greasy, slippery deck.

In the evening, an accident occurred to our surgeon, which, fortunately, did not seriously injure
him, although he was much shaken. In one of the
heavy lurches made by the ship he "fetched way," and
in falling, his head struck the end of a gun-carriage
with such force that, when picked up, he was quite
insensible, and covered with blood. He was immediately put into a cot on the main deck, and in
about half an hour regained his senses. On coming
to, he was quite unaware of the blow he had received, though the cut on his head and general
shaky feeling soon explained to him what had occurred. It was some days before he could leave his
bed and resume duty.

On the 28th, the weather had moderated so considerably that it was thought advisable to use
steam. The temperature was rising daily, and we
all felt the comfort of exchanging the cold northern
for the more temperate southern winds.

Our anchor was dropped off Nassau on the 2nd
of December, but did not, unfortunately, remain
very long at the bottom, as I will presently explain.

Shortly after our arrival, the Governor and four

of the Council came off to learn what arrangements were to be made for the Prince's landing. I do not wish to speak evil of dignities, but really truth compels me to say that they did not look nearly dignified enough for the onerous positions of Governor and M.PP. of the capital of the Bahamas. The look of wonder which landsmen almost always assume on coming on board a man-of-war was clearly visible on the faces of these gentlemen, and did not, perhaps, add to their importance; such at least was the opinion of our youngsters, though, by the bye, I never yet came across any rank, however exalted, which would secure respect from the larking inhabitants of a gun-room mess—of course I mean when by themselves.

The Nassau papers had for some days been filled with " proclamations," " notices," and " gazettes extraordinary" relative to the ceremonies, illuminations, &c. which were to take place on the landing of the Prince. The broadsheet of the *Bahama Herald*, of which I have now a copy before me, consists of sixteen columns of type, of which six are letterpress, the remainder being devoted to advertisements. One of these latter is occupied by the all-pervading Holloway, whose wonderful cures are published therein at length, to the great benefit, I should imagine, of the editor of the paper, if not to the edification of the Bahama public at large.

o 2

It was a matter of much regret to most of us that we did not go ashore at the same time as His Royal Highness; as, supposing that we could land just as easily " to-morrow," all but two of the officers put off their visit to the town till that proverbially disappointing period. The sort of to-morrow which we expected never came. The Prince, Captain, and Major Cowell embarked for the shore in a large schooner yacht which had been placed at their disposal; but their proceedings, the aspect of the town, and its inhabitants, &c. &c. cannot be recorded for the following reason.

During the night it came on to blow heavily, and when morning broke, a signal was observed hoisted on shore directing us to weigh and proceed to *South-West Bay*, there to remain until calmer weather should render it possible to return to our anchorage, which was none of the safest in such a breeze, though the best to be found off that part of the island.

Now, we had taken on board a pilot, one of the most knowing of men in his own peculiar profession, who, on being told that he was to take the ship to the above-named anchorage, declined to do so; but recommended that, as our present position was unsafe, the ship should be taken to South-West Bay, Abaco Island. Thither we accordingly steamed; and after about five hours' run, found ourselves at anchor off the uninteresting neighbourhood of Abaco

Lighthouse—the only sign of habitation visible on the island from our point of view.

Meantime the people of Nassau, imagining that we had proceeded to the bay originally intended, had sent round carriages, horses, &c., to provide for our conveyance to the town in order to be present at the ball about to be given in the evening in honour of the Prince ; and the astonishment of all parties was great when no *St. George* made her appearance, and, as a matter of course, the carriages returned with no other occupants save their disappointed drivers.

This then was the reason why none of us, save two, visited Nassau. During our stay at Abaco, which lasted two days, M—— and myself landed to see what sort of place the island was, and to try our luck at shooting. We speedily satisfied ourselves on the former head ; and with respect to sport, seagulls and turkey buzzards (or birds much resembling them) were the only specimens of the feathered creation which came within range of our fowling-pieces. We picked up, however, some splendid specimens of *sea-fans*, of a bright yellow and beautiful purple colour, which almost rewarded us for our excursion.

Getting off to the boat again (pinnace) was by no means an easy job. We were ultimately obliged to strip to the waist to avoid wetting our clothes, carrying our unmentionables, shoes, stock-

ing, and bundles of fans on the tops of our heads;
in this picturesque attire, we managed to climb
over the bows of the boat, barking our shins
severely in the operation.

The old pilot noticed above deserves special
mention. He was a nice old man, very nice.
Just one of those quiet looking parties who look as
if they could no more do any particular harm than
fly. But our boatswain, an old West Indian
stager, had a dim recollection of a certain captain
of a slaver (some people said pirate vessel) which a
few questions converted into a certainty. But the
captain alluded to was known some three-and-
twenty years ago, and had since disappeared from
public notoriety. Besides, it's ill work raking up
old stories to a person's disadvantage, and charity is
a great virtue. So the boatswain, like a prudent
man, held his tongue, made no allusion of an
unpleasant nature to hemp or cold steel, and
allowed us, while the old party was on board, to
take him on his own merits, such as they appeared
to be.

All sailors admire a man who can spin a good
yarn; and certainly our pilot extorted admiration
from all of us in this way. I always thought myself, that a Yankee was the best hand at telling a
" good 'un," that the world produces; but on this
occasion, the toughest to swallow that ever
emanated from a down-easter was eclipsed by our

nautical friend. The gravity with which he came
out with twister after twister, the look of innocence
with which he accompanied their recital, and the
indignant way in which he repudiated any insinua-
tion that their veracity was questionable, beat " all
creation." I did not, unfortunately, note down
enough of our conversation to recall many which
sorely taxed my risible muscles to avoid laughing
in his face, but one or two I do recollect.

One evening he was seated with myself and two
or three others on the main deck, smoking. I had
heard of his yarn-spinning qualifications, and was
anxious to find out if the current report of them
had been exaggerated, so I led the conversation to
sharks. Now sharks are to the sailor, as all the
world knows, what tigers are to the Indian officer,
or lions to the Cape settler—viz., an inexhaustible
source of stories, good, bad, and indifferent.

After a few general remarks, I mentioned a story
which had been told me by Mr. E——, our carpenter, who assured me that he could vouch for its
truth. Had it come from a stranger, however, I
should have hesitated to have implicitly believed
it; at all events, I calculated on surprising the
pilot. It was to the effect that some five or six
years before, Mr. E—— had belonged to a ship in
which they caught an immense shark. As usual,
after he had been disabled, he was cut open, and
the effluvium which proceeded from his interior

was so strong that no one could approach him.
Sure, however, from previous experience, that this
odour could only proceed from some animal matter
in the stomach, some of the men were induced to
proceed in the work of exploring the monster, and
the result of their labours was the exhumation of
three human skulls, and nearly all the bones complete
of as many bodies.   The surgeon of the ship
endeavoured to preserve the skulls, but decomposition was too far advanced, and he was obliged to
consign them the second time to the deep whence
they had so strangely been brought to light.

The pilot heard me without betraying the
slightest sign of astonishment, merely remarking
that he knew a more wonderful case, similar in
many respects, which had occurred in the very bay
where the ship had been anchored.   We pressed
him to tell us all about it; so he began.

" Well, about a year ago " (here he took a long
draw at the pipe and paused reflectively).

" What happened ? " said I.

" There was a boat capsized on the bar."   (Puff,
and pause again.)

" Ah, how did that happen ? go a-head, old
chap."

" Don't you hurry a man when he's telling a
story."   (Another pause of much longer duration
than the previous one.)

At last, however, he got fairly under weigh, and

(barring rather long intervals for draws at the pipe and reflection, or invention maybe) told the following yarn.

Some twelve months ago, a boat containing seven individuals was capsized in the surf off the bar at Nassau. Every one of the unfortunate crew were drowned, including the coxswain, who was a white man, and who had, at the time of the accident, a watch in his pocket which was going. The wretched blacks were seen to disappear one by one from the surface of the water, while the fins of some huge sharks swimming round the spot but too clearly indicated their doom. Last of all, the white coxswain disappeared, and for some days nothing was heard of the bodies, nor were any remains found of the victims.

About five days afterwards, a merchantman laying , in the harbour caught an immense shark—so large indeed, that great wonder was expressed at its size and weight. On being opened, the stench was so powerful that one man fainted right off, and the same result nearly followed with another on the contents of his maw being exhibited. *Seven skeletons, ranged in regular order like sardines in a tin case*, met the astonished gaze of the captors; and sticking to the ribs of one—the white coxswain— was the identical silver-cased watch he used to wear, *still going ! ! !*

How the pilot got over the watch part of the

business I do not know, as he made a slight error
in calculation, considering that few watches will go
forty-eight hours, and five days had elapsed before
the shark was caught.   He was terribly annoyed,
however, when we pointed this out, doggedly
repeating " Well, I tell you it is a fact—a *fact*,
sir.".

We were quite satisfied with this specimen of his
powers of invention.   The only other story I recollect at this moment, was one in which a shark got a
mortal disease from eating off the ends of some oars
which had been newly coppered.   I forget particulars, but he asserted the fish in question to have
exceeded forty-five feet in length.

The departure of the old gentleman was profoundly regretted, a living Baron Munchausen
being a rarity on board ; however, he left some
useful hints behind him.

Before I quit the subject of sharks, I will relate
one or two yarns whose recital was the consequence
of the above story.   As I can vouch for *them*, it
will be only necessary to premise that the parties
mentioned are now living.

All readers of naval books will recollect the story
of the slaver being condemned through papers found
in a shark's stomach, she having thrown them overboard on being boarded by a cruiser, and one of
these fish, seeing a delicious morsel, as he imagined,
having snapped up the bundle and been afterwards

captured by the identical cruiser. But I do not know that any one was ever in greater danger (unless actually immersed) while catching a shark, than the hero of the following story.

"Some time ago," said he, " I belonged to a ship on this station, and one day had made several unsuccessful attempts to tempt the palate of a large shark who was amusing himself under our stern. Vainly did I offer him tender pieces of salt beef or pork—the brute was not hungry, and was not to be tempted. I was determined to have him somehow, so I went below and took a fair sized salmon, which I had caught on shore, and placed it on the hook. Over both hook and fish I tied an old white shirt, and thus armed returned to the quarter boat whence I had been fishing, and lowered the apparatus into the water. In so doing I carelessly stood in the centre of the coil of a one and a-half inch rope which formed my line. Scarcely had the bait reached the water than the fish darted at it, and before I well knew what was- the matter, the coil tautened round my legs, and I was dragged partly over the gunwale of the boat, just managing to catch hold of the davit with both hands to save myself from going overboard completely.

" My situation was not pleasant. There I was at an angle of forty-five degrees, all my joints stretched to their utmost tension by the rope, which slowly rendered round my legs, barking them frightfully

in various places. The shark was evidently determined to have his pull out, and I began to feel as
if I could hold on no longer, when my calls for
assistance, which had been pretty vigorous, brought
the quartermaster to my aid, who finally released
me from my unpleasant position—not, however,
until I had learned to fully appreciate the sort of
agony inflicted by the rack, though in my case the
pain was comparatively light."

Mr. K——, our boatswain, told me that while
laying at Beyrout, he saw a shark caught which
contained in its stomach an entire child, so recently
swallowed, that decomposition had not even commenced. He also mentioned another story about a
soldier of the regiment stationed at Corfu some four
years since, who had all the flesh stripped from the
bones of one leg by a shark, and who actually
survived the horrible mutilation. " But enough of
shark stories," my naval reader will say, " I can tell
better myself." Perhaps you can, so I cry *peccavi*,
and will "return to our muttons," or rather our
anchorage off Nassau, whither we returned on the
6th December.

The Prince came on board in the afternoon, as
did also F—— and M——, who had landed previous to our being obliged to weigh. They gave a
most glowing description of the town, and the
balls, &c., given by its hospitable inhabitants. It
is very strange, but so sure as one stayed away

from anything of the kind that was given during
our cruise, just as certainly it was described by
those who went to it as the best ball, &c., that they
had ever attended. So it was in the present case,
and our shipmates' description of the proceedings at
Nassau did not by any means tend to console us for
our absence from them.

I have above stated that I am unable to give,
from personal observation, any particulars of the
island ; but if my readers will pardon my again
quoting the daily press, they will gain some idea of
the welcome accorded to the Prince, by perusing
the subjoined paragraphs which have come into my
possession since the former part of this chapter was
written—

" BAHAMA HERALD.— *Wednesday, December* 4, 1861.

" Her Majesty's steamship *St. George,* having on
board His Royal Highness Prince Alfred, was
signalled on Monday, about twelve o'clock, and
about three, came to anchor off Hog Island. The
St. George's Cross was then hoisted as a signal that
His Royal Highness was on board. The committee deputed for that purpose, then went on
board, and ascertained that His Royal Highness
would land at eleven o'clock yesterday. All hands
were busily set to work to finish the preparations
which were being made for his reception, and
which, we think, considering the time allowed,

none can find fault with. Accordingly, at an
early hour yesterday, all were busily astir to
witness this first visit of royalty to our little
island ; and by ten o'clock, all the windows in Bay
Street were thronged with fair faces, anxiously
looking out for signals of his approach. The seats
prepared for visitors at the Public Abutment were
not quite as well filled up as we expected they
would have been, from the number of tickets given
out, and we noticed, notwitstanding it was strictly
prohibited, the admittance of several children, even
under the age of six years. Knowing many who
had been deterred from coming with theirs in consequence of such an arrangement, we really think
the order issued should not have been allowed
to have been infringed upon by any one. By
eleven o'clock all was prepared, and on the firing of
the guns from the *St. George* (as well as those from
Fort Charlotte) announcing His Royal Highness
having left the ship, all eyes were anxiously strained
to catch the first glimpse of our noble sailor Prince,
who no sooner came in sight, than he was greeted
with deafening cheers, and the waving of hats and
handkerchiefs from the assembled crowd. When
the boat reached the wharf a royal salute was fired
from the barracks by the Royal Artillery, and upon
landing, His Royal Highness was received upon the
platform by the Lieutenant-Governor, the Chief
Justice, the members of the Executive Council, and

the Colonel Commandant, which gentlemen were
presented to the Prince and an address delivered to
His Royal Highness by the Lieutenant-Governor."

Then follows a list of the persons presented to
H.R.H., which would of course be extremely uninteresting to the general reader.

"In the afternoon his Royal Highness, attended by
Major Cowell, took a drive to the eastward, gratifying those who were unable to attend in the morning
with a sight of his person ; and in the evening he
drove through the town to witness the illuminations
in the carriage of the Honourable W. H. Doyle,
guarded by two policemen on either side.

"A word more as to the decorations.   The arches
erected by Messrs. Squires and Nicolls do them
infinite credit and are very tasteful.   The seats at
the public abutment are exceedingly comfortable
and very nicely arranged.   Mr. Samuel Whiting,
American Consul, deserves much praise for the very
great loyalty displayed in all his arrangements, and
the entwining of the American and English flags
across the street was . fully emblematical of his
wishes for the perfect unanimity of both countries.

"Flags were displayed from all the vessels in the
harbour, and we could not help noticing the very
loyal feeling shown by Mr. Charles Hall, from his
little schooner of six tons, named the *Independence*.
Her yards were manned and she fired guns as the

Prince was passing, making even some of the larger
vessels look rather small.

" The illuminations were very general and exceedingly tasteful.   In the centre of the Court House
was displayed the royal arms with the initials V.
and A. on either side, surrounded by a half circle
of " WELCOME," and having underneath another semi-
circle of the Rose, Shamrock, and Thistle entwined,
as well as a number of brilliant lights from each
window, and several coloured ones, suspended from
the trees in front.   Over the boat-house belonging to
the Customs was a very pretty design ; " WELCOME,
SAILOR PRINCE," was placed in a circle with an
anchor in the centre, and underneath the word
" CUSTOMS " was placed.   The yacht *Georgina*, and
several of the other vessels in the harbour, were very
prettily lighted.   Government House had several
coloured lights suspended from the gate up to the
house, which was also very brilliantly lighted up.
At a little after eight a company of the Royal Field
Artillery were stationed at respective distances in
front of the gate, holding blue lights, which while
they lasted had a very pretty effect.   The Hotel
showed itself off to very great perfection ; the
numerous, and admirable arrangement of the lights
displayed the beauty of the building to very great
advantage.   Expecting to see something worthy of
note from the Barracks and Officers' Quarters, we
walked as far as the Town Parade ; to our surprise,

however, both those sides of the Square were dark
as midnight, though Mr. Dronet's house on the
opposite side looked very brilliant. The illuminations from the American Consul's were in equal good
taste with his other preparations. The transparen-
cies in front of his piazza had the word " Welcome"
in a circle at the top, underneath which was

> We love thy Mother, and accord to one
> So dear to her a proper homage due,
> May QUEEN VICTORIA'S noble SAILOR-SON,
> Be like his Sovereign Mother, good and true.

Under that was " A Sailor's welcome to a Sailor's
Prince." All looked very pretty.

" Several rockets were sent off from the barracks
and public buildings in the course of the evening ;
but were we to enumerate the many other things
worthy of notice which came under our eye, we fear
this would necessarily have to be a Thursday instead of a Wednesday evening's issue ; our readers
will therefore, we trust, be content with what we
have already furnished them, and we feel quite sure
we are safe in asserting that our Royal Prince's visit
will be long remembered by every inhabitant in
Nassau.

" His Royal Highness took a ride out this morning, and this afternoon attended the parade on horseback, accompanied by Major Cowell, R.E., the garrison Staff, Dr. Duncombe, Staff-surgeon of the New
Providence militia, and His Excellency's private

P

secretary. His Royal Highness was received on
the ground by Lieutenant-Colonel Whitfield, commanding the troops, to whom he presented a new
set of colours for his regiment; but time will not
admit of our giving the particulars until our next
issue, when they shall appear in full length. To-
night, we understand, he attends a ball at Govern-
ment-house; to-morrow night one at the Court-
house. Many ladies; hearts we have no doubt are
palpitating until both are over."

———

"*ADDRESS of Lieutenant-Governor to His Royal
Highness Prince Alfred Ernest Albert, on landing
at Nassau, N.P., 3rd December*, 1861.

"To Prince ALFRED ERNEST ALBERT.

"May it please your Royal Highness.

"The anticipation of the arrival of the noble ship
St. George with your Royal Highness in the clear
waters that lave the coral reefs and shady shores of
the Bahamas, and its submarine gardens, teeming
with animal and vegetable life of great beauty, variety, and utility, had already caused a thrill of
enthusiastic delight among all classes residing in
this remote western maritime colony of the British
Empire, enjoying, under her Majesty's powerful
protection, the inestimable blessings of peace, freedom, and security.

"First discovered by the immortal Columbus, this

cluster of rocky islands largely fulfilled the hope
of that renowned discoverer, and revealed a New
World, over a large portion of which the English
language, race, and civilization have since extended.

"The advent of the second son of our beloved
Queen at Nassau, the metropolis of this ancient and
loyal colony, has filled the hearts of the people with
joy, and is another important event in Bahama
history, of which its inhabitants will be ever proud;
and, it is my high and gratifying privilege, as Lieutenant-Governor, on behalf of myself, the consti-
tuted authorities, and the public, to greet your
Royal Highness on landing with a cordial welcome
to the Bahamas, and to express the anxious desire
of the inhabitants generally to render your auspi-
cious visit agreeable to yourself, and satisfactory to
our august Sovereign."

Such being the feeling of the colonists, as set
forth in the above extracts, it is not to be wondered
at that few more pleasant visits were made by the
Prince than that to the capital of the Island of New
Providence. This was the last visit which he paid
officially to our transatlantic colonial possessions,
though our cruise lasted for some little time longer.

After leaving Nassau (18th Dec., 1861) we
touched at the island of Mariguana; the only interesting circumstance connected with which place

is the fact, that although anchored in five fathoms
water, the depth under our stern was one hundred
and twenty fathoms, the anchor having been dropped
just on the edge of a perpendicular bank.   This
place formerly possessed an unenviable notoriety as
being the resort of pirates, who cruised in and out
of the numerous passages and channels of these
widely scattered islands, plundering or doing worse
when opportunity offered.   Of course this has long
been put a stop to, but I can easily imagine that
even at the present day a bold clever man might
easily, for a time, carry on a well-organized system
of piracy without detection, using one of these
islands as a rendezvous, though of course eventual
capture would be certain.

Finding on our arrival at Mariguana that orders
had been left us to proceed to Port Royal, we left
for that place on the 17th and arrived there on the
19th December, 1861.

NOTES ON CHAPTER XIII.

The discovery of the Bahamas, the first land seen by Columbus
in his search for a western passage to the Indies, is thus related
by Martin : (p. 4.)

" He thought it probable that they would make land that
very night, and therefore ordered a vigilant look-out to be kept
from the forecastle, promising a doublet of velvet to the person
who should first descry the shore, in addition to the pension of
10,000 maravedis guaranteed by the sovereigns.   The greatest
excitement prevailed, and not an eye closed on board the little

squadron on that eventful night. The breeze freshened and the vessels were ploughing the waves at a rapid rate, when the admiral, seated on high and scanning the western horizon in deep anxiety, thought he beheld a light glimmering in the distance. Fearing that it was but a vision conjured by his eager hopes, he called to Pedro Gutierrez—a gentleman of the king's household—who saw it likewise. The transient and uncertain gleams soon disappeared, and all was again doubt and uncertainty, until two a.m., when Martin Pingon, who was ahead of the admiral, fired a gun—the joyful signal that land was in sight. The vessels shortened sail and lay to, awaiting the dawn ; Columbus, his officers, and seamen, remaining meanwhile in a state of tumultuous delight which no other persons have probably ever experienced.

" With the morning light the voyagers beheld for the first time a portion of the western world, a level, thickly-wooded island, several leagues in extent, with numerous inhabitants perfectly naked, and gazing with astonishment on the vessels. Dressed in scarlet and bearing the royal standard he hastened on shore, fell on his knees, kissed the earth, and returned thanks to God with tears of joy. His example was quickly followed by his companions, who, recently so mutinous, now thronged around him, embraced his feet, and bursting into extravagant transports, gave themselves up to unbounded joy."

The island in question was called by the natives *Guanahané*, and is now generally known by the name of *Cat Island*.

The natives watched with astonishment the ceremonial of taking possession of the island. Little knowing the fearful consequences involved to themselves by this apparently harmless proceeding, they treated their visitors with every hospitality, believing them to be visitors from the gods.

The following is the description given by Martin of the aborigines :—

" They were well made, of a copper hue, and had long black hair, broad and lofty foreheads, remarkably fine eyes and pleasing features, though obscured and disfigured by paint. Their canoes—some capable of containing forty-five men—were dexterously managed with paddles : they had no iron, their lances being pointed with flint or fish bone; and few objects of barter, except tame parrots, large balls of cotton yarn, and a kind of bread called cassava, prepared from a large root named ' yuca,' which they cultivated."

The Lucayan Islands (so called it is supposed from *Los Cayos*, the Keys) were discovered on the 11th October, 1492. Within fifteen years, it is stated, no less than 40,000 of these unoffending people were transported to Hayti as slaves, to fill the vacancies caused by the rapid decrease of the aboriginal Haytians, from the tyrannical conduct of the Spanish colonists, whose fiendish cruelties excited the indignant abhorrence of Las Cases and many of his contemporaries.

" The Bahama Islands are the least interesting and least valuable part of the archipelago. The group consists of about 500 islands, many of them mere rocks, lying east of Cuba and the coast of Florida. Twelve are larger and cultivated, producing logwood and mahogany. The most intricate labyrinth of shoals and reefs, chiefly of corals, madrepores, and sand, encircle these islands ; some of them rise to the surface, and are adorned with groves of palm trees. The Great Bahama is supposed to be the first part of the New World on which Columbus landed. The next was Hayti."—Somerville's *Physical Geography* (p. 122.)

215

CHAPTER XIV.

On our arrival for the second time at this well-known harbour we found her Majesty's ships *Conqueror, Sanspareil, Mersey,* and *Donegal,* at anchor; the three former having on board portions of the detachment of Royal Marines destined to act in combination with the French and Spanish forces in the operations about to be undertaken against the Mexicans at Vera Cruz.

We were much pleased at the idea of active service. Hitherto indefinite reports alone had reached us relative to the part taken by England in this affair, and we had been rather sceptical of any definite result accruing from the much talked-of convention. But here were ships and here were men; besides that, our Armstrong guns had arrived in the *Mersey,* and were on the morning following our arrival transferred to us in exchange for an equal number of the old pattern. Things in general looked war-like, and the more sanguine among those on board began to indulge in visions of naval brigades and other expeditions, which would give them an idea of service rather different to that in which we had been engaged during the first part of our commission.

We received from the *Conqueror* five officers and one hundred and fourteen men. Of the former, I can only say that a jollier set of fellows never existed than our temporary shipmates; and the latter conducted themselves during the whole period of their stay on board in a way which called forth the highest expression of approval from those in authority.

The French squadron destined for the expedition arrived and anchored a few hours after ourselves. It was commanded by Admiral Jurien de la Graviére, whose name has become famous in naval circles from his work on the Navies of England and France, in in which their respective merits are discussed with much ability, and, for the most part, impartiality. He left, with the ships under his command, the following day. The *Donegal* and *Conqueror* also took their departure for the northward, and the *Mersey* and *Sanspareil* sailed for the rendezvous off Cape San Antonio, Cuba, leaving us to follow as soon as we had completed our preparations for sea.

I found my few acquaintances at Port Royal much as I had left them. Especially was I pleased to find that my friend B—— of the Naval Hospital had survived the sickly season, and was looking as jolly

as possible, pretty well reconciled by this time to his
exile from England—for residence at such a place
must be exile indeed.

There is nothing more to be said about Port Royal
than that contained in previous chapters. Land
crabs, blacks, earthquakes, hurricanes, and all those
things for which not only Port Royal, but Jamaica
in general are celebrated, having to the best of my
ability, been fully discussed therein; so we will now
bid adieu to the place with a most devout wish on
my part that I may never see it again. Twice in a
lifetime being quite sufficient for me, and I think I
may add for most in the profession.

Christmas-day came, as do most in this part of
the world, accompanied with the usual amount of
sun and mosquitoes. There is something so utterly
foreign and un-English in a broiling hot twenty-
fifth of December, that one instinctively recognises
on this day, of all others in the year, the fact of
being absent from dear old England; and all the
friends and associations whose presence, to most, from
earliest childhood has accompanied the advent of
this joyous festival of our Church. No snow-covered
roofs or whitened branches; no glittering hoar frost
on the hard crisp ground; no bright berried holly or
venerable mistletoe greeted one's eyes on rising in
the early morning. Instead of the rural sights and
sounds of home, the down-pouring sun on the
smooth glassy surface of the harbour, (the monotony

of which was only broken by the fin of an occasional shark, or the plash of a nigger's paddle propelling his " dory,") the feathery cocoanut or palm tree growing on the point, waving in the light breeze, and the mountains visible in the distance, looking like the water around us, of that deep blue which land or water either only can beneath a tropic sky—these were the natural accompaniments of the great day of the Nativity in the harbour of a West Indian island.

I am not given to suffering from *mal-du-pays* often, but certainly did feel home-sick on this day ; and no doubt many a homeward thought, and pleasant memory of byegone Christmases, passed through the minds of my fellow shipmates also as they recollected that this was Christmas-day.

But if the surrounding scenery was not calculated to bring the date to mind, we did by no means forget it. On that day we all seemed to feel that it was our duty to be merry ; kind words and kind looks abounded more freely as we wished each other many happy Christmas-days to come ; and in good time we observed the festivities of · the season, though the forenoon had to be devoted to work.

It was impossible (owing to our having to weigh) to perform divine service. We cleared the harbour about half-past eleven, a.m., and took our last look at Port Royal—few, I can safely say, regretfully.

As soon as we were well clear of the land, and the ship had resumed her wonted order, the crew, leave being granted, commenced keeping up Christmas in their own way. And a very noisy, jolly, and laughable way that was. In the first place, the lower deck messes had been duly decorated for the occasion, according to the taste and fancy of their respective members—a taste which was, occasionally, oddly manifested. The most popular description of ornament took the form of huge chandeliers, gorgeously bedecked with tinsel and coloured papers. They were constructed of iron or wooden hoops, their interiors, in most cases, tenanted by sugar or waxen angels (at least, Jack's idea of an angel), or tissue paper balloons—the latter pretty, but dangerous, being somewhat given to catching fire if not carefully watched. Trophies of flags, whose patterns were not to be found in any known signal book; pictures from the illustrated papers; and various other materials of decorative. art (many highly creditable to their designers) were pressed into service to give a gala-day appearance to the lower deck.

Of course every mess had its " Plum Duff" (or should it be *dough ?*), and, equally a matter of course, nearly every officer who made his appearance below was pressed to taste it; then, too, it was a *sine qua non* that the victim who had consented to be crammed with pudding, should take "just a sip of grog" to wash it down. Jack's hospitality on festive occasions is unbounded; only he forgets that stomachs are not made of india-rubber, but really feels offended if the proffered eatable is not stowed away therein. I am not in the secrets of the Doctor's books, but should imagine that there was a brisk demand for medicine of a certain kind next day. I wish we had had a few schoolboys on board to experimentalize upon; for if I recollect rightly, their appetites are generally unappeasable, in the way of plum-pudding, on shore.

But the great event of the day was the chairing. Few of the officers escaped this distressing honour; and rival parties, each headed by its own particular band, came into collision occasionally in a way which, though very laughable to a looker-on, must have been particularly unsatisfactory to the parties undergoing the operation. Most of the processions were headed by the fife and drum band; those containing the higher rank of officers being distinguished by the ship's band instead. Volunteer guards fell in on the upper deck to assist in the installation on the grating of those whom Jack more particularly delighted to honour.

The procession round the quarter deck and forecastle was all very well, and did not particularly inconvenience the party carried; but when it came to going down the hatchway to reach the main deck, the face of the individual on the chair assumed,

in most cases, an expression similar to that seen in
a man's face when the dentist is inserting his instrument to extract a tooth. For there was the
square of the hatchway, which was sharp and hard
at its lower edge ; and there were some dozen men
all trying to get down the ladder at once, still
bearing on high their unfortunate charge ; so that
a sort of wriggle was necessary to pass between the
edge of the hatchway and the top of the grating,
for the bearers never stopped, but proceeded on
their way, keeping time to the music, as if the
person they were conveying had not either a head
to be knocked or a body to be jammed. One officer,
whose height exceeded the usual stature, *did* get
stuck ; but his bearers took no notice of his position, but went ahead in the most cheerful way
imaginable, thereby nearly dislocating his neck or
fracturing his jaw. How he escaped either the one
or the other fate, I do not know. On the main
deck it was worse still. Bump went one's head
against beam after beam, the performance being
occasionally varied by the chair slipping either its
fore or hind legs through the holes in the grating,
thereby precipitating its occupant into the arms of
his guard of honour, who replaced him in his former
position very much in the same way in which a
child will replace its doll on a toy chair.

How we laughed, to be sure ! Between laughing
and cheering, I very soon had a splitting headache,

and was glad to go below and lie down, though the lively airs played by our first cornet effectually prevented sleep.

At half-past four, p.m., the men were told that their amusements must cease, in order to allow them time to prepare for evening quarters. Very much to the credit of the ship's company, two cases only of a "drop too much" were reported—a small percentage out of 800 people. The men returned to their duty in good spirits, delighted with their afternoon's fun, and in good working order, which I think decisively proves that a little licence occasionally will never, under proper regulations, interfere with the efficiency of a good ship's company.

We had a very jolly dinner below. Songs were sung, yarns spun, &c.; and we, in a quieter way, enjoyed ourselves in the evening as the ship's company had in the afternoon. Amongst the stories I heard, I cannot resist relating the following, although I have before told one or two on the same subject.

Sir John —— was some years ago Governor of Jamaica, and had amongst his numerous friends one whose capabilities as a teller of "tough yarns" were well known in the circle in which he moved. Now Sir John —— was particularly anxious to "bring him out" on one occasion for the benefit of a third party, and invited him to dinner for the purpose; but it happened that he had been made aware of the Governor's intention, and determined to " sell" him.

During the meal the conversation, as had been previously arranged, turned upon sharks.

"By the bye," remarked the Governor, "you, Mr. ——, have met with some remarkable adventures with those creatures, have you not?"

" Oh yes," replied the gentleman addressed, " but I do not like telling those stories ; they are so very strange that people who do not know me might doubt my veracity."

" Well, you know, of course, that that would not be the case with either of us," said the Governor with a wink to his friend, "so pray tell any you may recollect."

"Oh, if you will be satisfied with my word, of course I cannot have any objection. I will tell you one. Some years ago, I was cruising off the harbour, and had for nearly an hour been vainly endeavouring to catch a huge shark which had been playing round us. In leaning over the gunwale of the schooner my watch fell from my pocket, and the chain breaking, it went overboard and was lost. As you may imagine, I concluded that I should never see it again as we were in about 100 fathom water."

" So I should imagine," interposed the Governor.

" Well, I was cruising over the very same spot

just three years afterwards, in fact my bearings
from the land were precisely the same as when previously there, so that I must have been within a
hundred yards of my old position, and at this very
hour (just the same time of day I lost my watch)
we caught an immense shark, evidently a very old
one. We got him on board, and cut him open,
and what do you think I found inside him Sir
John?"

"Your watch," exclaimed the Governor and his
friend both at once.

"No, Sir John, *nothing but guts.*"

The Governor was "sold."

But to return to our own proceedings. It was
voted by both messes that we should have a snapdragon in honour of the day. Just fancy to yourselves, some five-and-thirty officers of ages varying
from forty-five to fifteen, all standing round a long
table awaiting the signal to begin a scramble for
burning raisins. Just fancy such a scene to yourselves, you young ladies of blushing seventeen, and
young gentlemen of the same age, who think you
are *too old* to join "the children" in the old Christmas game of snapdragon. We had no such
scruples, I can assure you, but set to work to burn
our fingers, and make our mouths uncomfortably
hot with burning spirits in a way that would not
have disgraced the merriest children's party that
was to be found in England on that identical

night; for as a great living author has well observed, " It *is* good to be children sometimes, and never better than at Christmas, when its mighty Founder was a child himself."

I am afraid, however, the snapdragon did not improve the French polish of the table, but that was a trifle.

And then the songs. C—— (one of the marine officers) gave us the " Young man from the country," which was loudly encored, and thoroughly appreciated by us, on account, I suppose, of the solemn warning which it contains against too great a partiality for pleasing young men from the rural districts, being so *very* applicable to ourselves.

Then we had a game at blindman's buff—hardly so amusing as that described by Dickens in his " Christmas Carol " as taking place at the house of Scrooge's nephew. But we managed to do a good deal of laughing notwithstanding, and turned in convinced that we had observed the convivialities of the season " as well as circumstances would admit, without inconvenience to the service."

We arrived at our appointed rendezvous on the 28th, and fell in with the squadron a short time afterwards. For three days we cruised in company till the appearance of the *Challenger*, bearing the broad pendant of Commodore Dunlop, who took us under his command, and proceeded to Vera Cruz.

A serious accident had very nearly happened

Q

during our three days' cruise. The *Sanspareil*, by some means, contrived one night to get her martingale over our taffrail; fortunately, no serious damage was done, beyond injuring the quarter davits on the port side, and considerably straining the stern-walk and iron work above it. Both sides do not always come off so easily when two line of battle ships come into such close proximity at sea.

We arrived at and anchored off the Island of Sacraficios, about four miles below Vera Cruz, on the 6th January 1862. H.M.S. *Jason* and a Spanish squadron were lying there, the French ships not having arrived.

CHAPTER XV.

THE appearance of Vera Cruz from our anchorage
at Sacraficios was very pleasing. Too far off to see
the injury done to its walls and buildings by the
effects of time, or the recent bombardment it sustained from the Americans, its skyline of roofs,
broken by many domes and minaret - looking
steeples, caused it to present more the appearance
of a town situated in an eastern country, than of
one existing in central America.

Opposite to the mainland lies the island fortress
of St. Juan de Ulloa, which is considered one of
the strongest of the fortifications of the place.
They had all been evacuated previous to our arrival,
to permit of their temporary occupation by the
Spanish general till the arrival of the allies.

Some sixty miles inland, forming a background
to the town and environs, is seen rising the magnificent snow-shrouded cone of Orizaba 17,374 feet in
height, with its ever fiery crater, which, seen like a

Q 2

star in the darkness of the night, has obtained for it the Mexican name of *Citlatepetl*—" The mountain of the star." It is one of the four volcanic peaks in the midst of which is situated, on a plain 7482 feet above the sea level, the capital of Mexico. After gazing at its white crest, rising majestically from the fog bank in which the lower part of the mountain was hidden, I could not help saying to myself " Now I have seen a mountain indeed." It ranks, I believe, about sixth among the mountain giants of the globe.

As I have before said, the Spanish commodore had already garrisoned the forts before our arrival ; he had also caused the town to be evacuated. As this step was taken without the consent, and in the absence of the French and English commanders, they were, as might have been expected, much annoyed at his precipitation. The policy which, as far as we were concerned, it had been our intention to pursue, was entirely opposed to that which he had followed—our object being merely to take possession of the forts, leaving the inhabitants of the town entirely unmolested, until satisfaction should be given for the outrages practised on British subjects, and arrangements made for the settlement of the debt due to Great Britain ; or, more correctly speaking, until it should have been paid in full— the value of Mexican promises being little, as past experience has taught us. But it was no part of

our plan to excite a dislike to ourselves in the minds
of the natives; in fact, so wretchedly were they
governed, that had our intentions been carried out,
we should most probably have been welcomed as
friends instead of being looked upon in a manner as
invaders.

Rumour—that mother of mischief—asserted that
the best feelings did not exist between the Spanish
powers and their allies. Whether this was the
case or not I am unable to say, but such was the
current report in the fleet. At all events, their
subordinates never omitted to pay the civilities
which that polite people seldom fail to render; so
we will presume that any feelings of the kind
alluded to, if they existed at head-quarters, did not
extend to those in a less influential position.

As for the Mexicans themselves, their hatred of
the Spaniards was only equalled by that proverbially
said to be entertained by the Prince of Evil for
holy water. I shall have occasion to notice this
subject in a future page. The French and ourselves
were decidedly popular, and would have been still
more so had it not been for the ill-judged proceedings
with respect to the occupation of the town by the
Spaniards above mentioned.

The French squadron, which we had previously
met at Port Royal, made its appearance at Sacraficios shortly after us; and for two or three days
the combined fleets, which included several trans-

ports, lay peacefully at anchor in the bay, anxiously
awaiting intelligence which should lead to some
movement on active service.   Various yarns relative
to what was to be done—naval brigades and ex-
peditionary detachments being landed, &c., &c.,
were of course flying about, and obtained credence,
more or less, according to the temperament of the
hearer.   During our stay no less than one hundred
Spanish sentries were brought in, who had been
shot at the outposts stationed outside the walls.
And so careful were the Mexican sharpshooters
to avoid detection, that to avenge their deaths was
a matter of impossibility.   They openly avowed
their intention of keeping up a guerilla warfare, in
the event of affairs terminating in an appeal to
arms ; and in such a country it would, I can easily
imagine, be the best to adopt.

A Spanish soldier was shot for desertion, in the
great square of the city, during the time we were
lying here.

But while we were thus impatiently awaiting the
commencement of hostile operations, the events of
one day changed our thoughts and our prospects.

One evening a steamer arrived, bringing Spanish
papers containing a strange paragraph.   It stated
that Albert, Prince Consort of our beloved Queen,
was dead !

The next day the sad news was confirmed, and
the intelligence was broken to Prince Alfred.   Of

his grief I have no right, in these pages, to speak. Each can imagine to himself the effect of such a blow as the loss of such a near and dear relative.

But I may mention its effect upon ourselves. At first it was utterly discredited by all on board, no intelligence of his previous illness having reached us. But I can truly say that, when convinced of its truth, we felt, in common with the highest and the lowest in the land, the irreparable loss to our Queen and country, of one who in every relation of life, social and public, had merited the esteem and reverence of not only the millions owning the sway of the British sceptre, but of all foreign nations also. Monuments may be erected to his memory ; but his name, needing them not, will, like that of Alfred the Great, ever remain a household word in the hearts and homes of Old England. Peace to the ashes of the noble dead !

In consequence of this intelligence the ship was moved down to Anton Lizardo, an anchorage some ten miles below Sacraficios, to avoid the visits of condolence which would have doubtless been paid to His Royal Highness, by the various officers commanding the foreign ships at Sacrificios. Such visits, at such a time, being, as can be easily imagined, distressing in the extreme.

After we had been lying at anchor for two or three days, a fishing party was allowed to land, it being well known that no danger whatever was to be apprehended from the Mexicans, as they repeatedly declared that they had no desire whatever to injure the English so long as they abstained from any hostile demonstration.

I would here add (which I should have previously stated) that the ministers of the three allied powers were already on their way towards the capital, for the purpose of entering into negociations which should obviate the necessity of spilling blood.

However, it would not have done to have landed unprepared for any contingency which might occur. So we mustered up our pistols and other arms, offensive and defensive, and placed in the cutter a sufficient number of rifles, with ammunition, to arm her crew in case of necessity. I was directed to try and ascertain whether any beef or other meat was to be obtained in a sufficiently large quantity to give the ship's company a day or two's fresh food; and also to make inquiries as to whether fruit, milk, or vegetables were to be obtained.

We landed right enough, and in a very short time fires were blazing merrily along the sea beach, marking the distance over which the sein was being hauled. Leaving nearly all hands at work, pulling, cheering, and laughing, as, ever and anon, some one would get a ducking, or some laughable incident occurred, I proceeded, in company with three brother officers and two stewards, along the beach. After walking about a mile we came up

with two peons and several little boys, who gazed
at us with unfeigned astonishment, evidently not
knowing whether to stay where they were or run
away ; by way of reassuring them we called out,
" *Somos amigos ; no tenga miedo*," (we are friends ;
do not be afraid), and entered into conversation with
them.

They seemed greatly relieved to find that we
were Englishmen, and not Spaniards. We made
the necessary inquiries, and, after a short palaver,
agreed to follow one of them to a rancho a little
distance inland, whose owner we were assured would
give us all the information of which we were in
search.

Such a colony as there was in the *ranchero's* hut,
I never in my life saw before. There were about six
old women, six young ditto, and children innumer-
able; while their fathers crowded round the door
and plied me with questions. Two rooms were the
only accommodation for this heterogeneous assemblage (for the pigs and poultry, as in " ould Ireland,"
formed part of the domestic establishment), and
how they managed affairs in the way of stowage I
really cannot say. The *Amo*, or master of the house,
told me that he could get some bullocks by eleven
the following day, and offered for sale about two or
three dozen chickens, a pig, and a pine apple. The
latter we devoured on the spot; the former purchased and bagged, but did not look upon the pig

as an eligible investment. So, after a short time,
we returned as we came, in Indian file, singing by
way of keeping step, to the evident amusement of
our copper-colour hided guide.

Between twelve and one o'clock next day, during
the dinner hour, a private, belonging to the marine
battalion on board, fell down dead in his mess.   A
post-mortem examination showed that disease of the
heart was the cause of his death.   In this climate
the preparations for paying the last services of
humanity to the deceased are obliged to be hurried
in a way which but ill accords with our home ideas
—twenty-four hours being usually the time which
elapses between death and burial.   In this case even
a shorter period was allowed.   The coffin which was
to contain him being prepared during the evening
by the carpenters of the ship, an attempt was made
to land in the pinnace at one of the little islands in
the bay, the following morning.   There was, however, such a heavy surf on, that it was found to be
impossible; and the boat accordingly returned,
bringing back with it the coffin, which was returned
to its old position on the main deck.

I was leaning over the nettings, watching the
boat as she unsuccessfully endeavoured to approach
the island, and the thoughts naturally suggested by
such a scene came into my mind.   How strangely
spun is the thread of human destiny !   Yesterday
this poor fellow was well and hearty, and had

apparently a good prospect of a long life—for he had made no complaint previously; and had one, like the witch of old, foretold to him just twenty-four hours before, that, ere the sun should have once more risen and set, he should be lying prone and stiff in the cold embrace of death; that his heart should have been taken from his body for surgical examination; and that, coffined the same evening, his remains should be laid in their last narrow home in the sandy spot of earth before us, washed by the waters of the great Gulf;—had any one, I say, foretold this to him, how devoid of probability would he have deemed such a prophecy!

Who he was, and whence he came, I know not. But doubtless he left some behind in whose memory he was dear, and whose sorrow at his loss was aggravated by knowing 'that his bones lay on a foreign strand, under a tropical sun, instead of beneath the shade of venerable trees in some country churchyard in dear old England. People may say it matters little where one's final resting-place may be; perhaps so, to the dead themselves; but the affection of survivors demands some memorial of their loss. And this is one of those universal feelings which pervades the breasts of civilized and uncivilized humanity alike; for scarcely does the world afford an instance of a tribe who do not reverence their dead, and who do not recognise in it a great mystery passing the comprehension of the sons of men.

A second attempt to land in the afternoon proved more successful; and our worthy Chaplain committed, with the usual rites, the body to the earth, there to rest "till the last trumpet shall sound, and the sea shall give up her dead."

But to return to more cheerful subjects. The following forenoon three of us landed in the cutter to make arrangements for getting the beef, &c. We found our worthy friend of the *rancho* in an evident quandary. When I asked him where the bullock was which he had promised to bring down to the beach, he said that he regretted to inform me that a proclamation from the Governor, forbidding, under stringent penalties, any provisions being furnished to the "armed ships which had made their appearance off the coast," had reached him only the previous evening, and that he dare not disobey it. "Now, señor," said I, "tell me truly, do you want to sell the beef and vegetables or not?"

"Oh yes, we want money above everything; all our property has been taken for the service of the State, and we have scarcely a single *onza* among us."

While we were talking, some twelve or fourteen Mexicans on horseback, armed with sabres and pistols, had made their appearance. They lifted their hats as they wished us *Buenos dias*, and seemed peaceably inclined; so we returned their salute, and for a few minutes the conversation became general.

"How many guns had our ship?—how many men?"—880.   "*Santissima Maria!   Ocho cientos ochenta hombres!*" (But they must require an immense quantity of provisions!)—Who was our Captain?   He must be very noble to command so great a ship;—and scores of similar questions and exclamations were poured into my ears on all sides (I say mine, as the others did not understand Spanish).

Watching an opportunity when the storm of talking was over, I beckoned my first acquaintance to walk along the shore for a short distance. When we were out of earshot, I said—

"You say, señor, that you have no objection to sell your bullock. Why not let me have it? You may be quite sure that we shall not inform the Government that you have sold it. Besides, it is but a very trifling affair after all."

"*Mire señor*, here is the proclamation; read it yourself;" and he handed me a dilapidated piece of whity brown paper, whereon was printed the ordinance of the Governor.

This interesting document, in addition to stating the levies and subscriptions required for "the service of the State," furthermore proceeded to say that whosoever should furnish arms, provisions, or aid of any description to the enemies of Mexico (they should rather have said the enemies of her Government), should be considered and treated as

a traitor; that his house should be razed to the
ground, all his effects confiscated, and he himself
suffer the extreme penalty of the law.

"Well, but *we* are not your enemies," I said.
" We are only here to add to the effect of the pro-
positions made by our minister. Besides," I added,
" if we were, we should not offer to buy beef of you;
we should take it, and you, too, if you objected."

" *Es verdad, señor;* you could do so, if you
chose, doubtless; but it is not that alone, for we
like the English, and would serve you, and are also
in great want of money. But see there," said he,
pointing to a Spanish frigate at anchor in the Bay,
"if those cursed Spaniards see you embarking any
provisions, they will think it safe to land themselves and take what they can; and they will
surely kill us and burn our cottages if they land
in force ; for, save the dozen armed men you see
here, we are unprotected."

" You don't seem to love the Spaniards much,"
I remarked.   " What would you have done to us
three here, if we had been of that nation instead of
Englishmen ? "

" Killed you all—if we could," was the laconic
response.

A pleasant prospect, thought I to myself, for the
officers of the frigate if they venture to land un-
armed.   " Is there no way," I presently said, " of
arranging this little matter."

" A thought has come into my mind, señor.   If you will land this evening after dark I will let you have whatever you require, beef, fowls, vegetables, or pines ; and then neither the Spaniards or my companions here will know anything of the matter. To tell you the truth, I misdoubt some of those near us, and am more afraid of their knowing it than of anything else ; for if they inform against me, I am a lost man."

" Well, I will tell the Captain what you say, and if he likes to let a boat land—*bueno*.   If not, I can't help it."

We then rejoined the others.   One of the horsemen was evidently superior in position to his fellows ; and although not addressed by any title, there was a certain respect in their manner of addressing him.   So I entered into conversation with him by regretting that circumstances prevented my obtaining what I had come on shore for. He answered politely that he was sorry he could not permit anything to be taken off to the ship, and after a few civil speeches on both sides, our talk turned upon the war and its prospects.

He displayed an amazing amount of impartiality in his statement of the causes which had led to the present crisis.   His account of the governing powers was very amusing, there being, as he said, more than one master, each going his own way to work. When I mentioned the Spaniards his eyes glistened.

"Listen, señor. We like you, and the French also, though, of· course, if you land to invade the country, we must do our duty and defend it. But as for those *dogs*, we will show no mercy to them if we meet them in the field. All communication with them is strictly forbidden. Nay, if one is known to have spoken to one at the outpost he is shot instantly ; though, thanks to heaven, we have managed to destroy nearly a hundred of the rascals by means of our sharpshooters."

"But how is it," I asked, "that your feeling against them is so strong ?"

"Señor," said he gravely, "many years ago we ejected them from the land which, by their cruelties and oppressions, they had shown themselves unfit to rule. But, besides that, look at home, answer me whether kindly feelings generally exist between a revolted colony and the mother country? For example, America and yourselves. Why, at this very moment—— "

"Well," said I, "there is certainly some little disagreement at present, but we are not so blood-thirsty as to want to exterminate each other."

"I can read, señor, and see the *Diario* of Havana, and our own papers frequently," he replied rather indignantly, alluding to the paragraphs from American papers, copied into those journals—some of them certainly of anything but a pacific tendency.

But we talked about a great many other things than politics. He cut down for us some magnificent prickly pears, which he showed us how to open properly. By the bye, he also told me that their juice made excellent red ink; and I verified his statement on returning to the ship, by making a bottle full of a liquid which was, at all events, a good substitute for it. All the notes to be found in these pages were written with prickly pear ink.

The sabres of the horsemen under the command of the *Capitan de Infanteria*—as I found his title to be—were, though of good steel, very roughly got up. On the blades were embossed two Spanish inscriptions, which may be rendered—

"DO NOT DRAW ME WITHOUT CAUSE.—DO NOT SHEATHE ME WITHOUT HONOUR."

Among the shells to be found on the beach, I noticed the shell whose inhabitant furnishes the celebrated Syrian purple. I am not aware of its scientific name, and do not intend consulting an encyclopædia to find out in order to persuade people that I do. This is the first place we have visited during our cruise where I have found this shell, and cannot say whether it is to be found at the West Indian Islands.

On my reporting, when we got on board, the result of my conversation with the *ranchero*, it was not deemed prudent to send a boat on shore after dark. We left the anchorage next morning under orders for Havana. As we steamed past the point where dwelt our friend, he was to be seen on horseback, standing up to his saddle in water as far out as the bank he was on admitted, vigorously waving a handkerchief or some such article, apparently in the vain hope of attracting the Captain's attention, and inducing him to lower a boat. He was no doubt considerably sold at not having been able to sell his beef and vegetables to those who would have honestly paid for them—and wished, I dare say, that, even with the fear of his Government and the Spaniards before his eyes, he had allowed us to take them in broad daylight. It comforts me greatly to think that there is little probability I shall ever see him again, as perhaps, considering himself an aggrieved party, he *might* be rude if we met.

The *St. George* lay to under the lee of Sacraficios, awaiting despatches for the Commodore. I forgot to mention, that before leaving Anton Lizardo we transferred our marine battalion to the *Desperate* sloop. From the officers we parted with sincere regret, a feeling which I think I may venture to say they reciprocated.

After waiting about four hours, the mails and despatches made their appearance, and with infinite pleasure we heard the order given to "Go a-head," and bade farewell to Mexico.

And so ended our share in the Mexican expedition.

CHAPTER XVI.

THE HAVANA.

As we approached the harbour of Havana, those of
us who had not previously visited this port looked
in vain for the entrance. Not that it is not visible
enough to those who are acquainted with the coast,
the lighthouse, and fort on the left hand being con-
spicuous landmarks; but most of us did not know
one end of the town from the other, nothing but a
mass of white buildings being distinguishable at ten
miles off—such being our distance from it when we
took the pilot on board.

As we got still nearer to the land the impression
made on our minds was not favourable. That it
was a large town was pretty evident, as also the fact
that the whitewasher's trade must be a profitable one,
as every house was white, which was not of some
other colour. (Do not laugh reader, I do not call
stone and brick facings *colours*. Blue, green, and
red *paint* are what I am alluding to.)

We all agreed that it was not half so picturesque

R 2

as Vera Cruz. No lofty domes or slender towers
broke the monotony of the roofs. Here and there
certainly might be seen a few church steeples, but
those visible were not, as a rule, remarkable for
architectural beauty. That the interior arrangements
might be infinitely superior to those of the Mexican
city we fully believed; but it is a pity that they could
not show more in the shape of outward beauty.

The pilot boarded us as above stated, when we
were about ten miles outside. Now, I have seen a
good many pilots of all nations—from the Chinese
pilot, whose unintelligible order in pigeon English,
"Shizzee main tawse," "(Shiver the main topsail,
alias put the ship about,") on one occasion delighted
me, being, as I then imagined, the first words of
pure Chinese I had ever heard spoken—to the portly
North Sea pilot of our own waters, whose innumer-
able coverings and heavy boots (which would inevit-
ably drown him if he fell overboard) must considerably increase the risk to his insurers. Each and all
were important men, both in their own and others'
estimation; but few showed it more unmistakably
than the well-to-do individual who took her Majesty's
ship *St. George* through the narrow entrance to
Havana Harbour, and finally anchored her within it.
He beat even the "Mudian" mentioned in a former
chapter, and he was "no small beer" either.

A mail was immediately brought off to the ship,
on our arrival, which contained letters bringing offi-

cial intelligence of the death of his Royal Highness
The Prince Consort. The *Donegal* (which line-of-
battle ship came in shortly after ourselves) and the
St. George, accordingly, on the following day, fired
funeral salutes, as did also the foreign men-of-war
present.

The *Donegal* brought us sad news. The splendid
Conqueror had been lost and was a total wreck on
one of the Bahaman Islands! Little did we think
when we last saw her at Port Royal that we were
taking our last look at one of the finest two deckers
in the service; yet so it was, and scarcely anything
was now left of the magnificent hull; the stores were,
however, most fortunately saved, and vessels had been
despatched to take them and her crew on board and
convey them to Bermuda. As the papers have so
very lately given full particulars of the wreck, I
will not further allude to it herein.

Now, before I begin to describe the Havana, let
me tell you that I have been reading Trollope's work
on the West Indies—not with a view to find out
what to say, but what *not* to say. As it so happens
that I differ very much in opinion on many points
with that gentleman (for whose powers I nevertheless entertain very great respect) such a course will
be easy. So now here goes—

First of all, then, we landed—such a proceeding
being indispensable when you are the inhabitant of
a floating residence—and the place where we landed

was the arsenal. If any of my readers are acquainted with the gun wharf at Portsmouth, let them divide the ground therein by thirty-six and they will get a fair idea of the area of this public establishment; passing through the gates of the said arsenal we found ourselves in the town at once.

The houses were very high and the streets very narrow, but that is on account of the sun I suppose. The roads were very dirty, but that was on account of the recent rain. One could put up with both of those little drawbacks, but we could not get over the pavements. You may take the phrase whichever way you will—metaphorically or literally. Two and a half feet is not sufficient width for the pavement of a street in a large city. Natives answer this objection by saying that none but dogs, niggers, and Englishmen ever dream of walking. Ladies, under no circumstances whatever. But I am sure I saw a great many who would have been equally insulted had either of the above terms been applied to them; for Cubans are very proud of their island. One thing is, that were the pavements wider, the carriage ways would be narrower, and there is no room to spare in them, so that it would be only "robbing Peter to pay Paul." Besides, they are making a move in the right direction in the more modern streets, while the squares absolutely luxuriate in pavement; so, perhaps, my complaint had better be modified.

Reader, have you ever wondered at the cabalistic
black marks on cigar boxes, on which fragments of
letters unite to inform you that "*Londres superiores*"
from the factory of Cabaña are the contents? I
have often done so; and for a long period remained
in a state of ignorance as to whether "Cabaña" was
an individual, a town, or a manufactory. When I
discovered that it was the name of the Prince of
cigar merchants, I became sceptical as to the mark
being in all cases *bonâ fide*. Cigars with a strong
suspicion of cabbage-leaf having been taken in my
presence from a box labelled in this way—though
perhaps they were not the original tenants—I always
looked upon the Cabaña mark as a pure imposition,
believing that it was possibly still used by cigar
merchants at home to delude the inexperienced into
the belief that they were purchasing foreign cigars.
I had seen this name everywhere. In China, in
Australia, in Halifax, in England—wherever civilization prevailed—there just as surely would one come
across a black branded mark on a box which was
undoubtedly the monogram of this wonderful man.

It was, therefore, with no small feelings of pleasure
that I entered the shop of Cabaña. Not that I saw
therein the man himself, he having long retired from
the cares of business, and, I think, of life also. But
the chief of the present firm was there, Señor de la
Valle, whose politeness was great. After seeing the
few thousand boxes which he kept there as a sort of

" present use store," we could well believe that the
branded boxes I have spoken of might well be the
exports of this wonderful factory.

As a great number of officers dealt very extensively
with Cabaña (for such we always called him, though
his name was Valle) in the manufactured weed, he
took great trouble to show us all that was interesting
connected with cigars. In the first place, let me tell
you, he scorns to deal in anything but them, and, in
fact, betrayed an ignorance on the subject of bird's-
eye and shag tobacco, which astonished me in a man
of his years. I do not think he ever smoked a pipe
in his life—always cigars. What an elysium of
smoke!

We asked to look at some of those weeds whose
fabulous prices had reached our ears, though we
never believed in their existence. Going to a glass
case, the señor produced therefrom a large-sized
cigar, which he handled with extreme delicacy and
care. " This cigar, gentlemen," said he, "is a
three hundred" (meaning three hundred dollars per
thousand, or fifteen pence each—a high price at
Havana). The precious article was handed from
one to the other, and having been duly inspected,
was returned to its niche in the glass case.

" And who buys these splendid specimens of the
manufacture?" we asked.

" Chiefly the crowned heads and higher nobility

of Europe; at the present moment we are making a number for the Emperor of Russia."

And so we looked in succession at specimens of cigars at all prices: the lowest sold were twenty dollars per thousand. He gave us a handful each of "*forties*," and we fully appreciated the gift.

I did not myself visit the manufactory, it being situated some distance outside the town; but I am indebted to a brother officer for the following description of it.

The cigars are made in the upper room of a long two-storied building, the ground-floor being devoted to the stowage of the plant itself. A great number of Chinamen are employed by Señor del Valle, and their plodding, persevering way of working enables them to become very skilled in the manufacture, which exactly suits the temperament of these sons of the Celestial empire. No one is allowed to smoke while working—a prudent precaution, as otherwise the three hundred dollar specimens would soon disappear. The leaf of which these *chefs d'œuvre* are made is of extremely fine texture, the ribs and stalk being very small. When held against the light it looks almost as clear as a piece of brown coloured glass.

The best cigars are made of one piece of the leaf; the inferior kinds being composed of odds and ends of leaves surrounded by the outside skin. There is

a deal of art in making a good article, and no doubt
the artistic element of beauty enters as largely into
the ideas of a proficient in cigar making as into
those of a porcelain manufacturer.

After so much about the smoking materials of
the present day, it is amusing to read the following
notice of their first discovery by Europeans:—

"Columbus would have thought it strange, indeed, could he have been told that a custom which
he and his sailors here watched with astonishment,
as a singular, unaccountable, and even nauseous
practice, would become common amongst every
civilized nation. They saw several Indians going
about with firebrands in their hands, and certain
dried herbs, which they rolled up in a leaf, and
lighting one end, put the other in their mouths, and
continued exhaling and puffing out the smoke. A
roll of this kind they called 'a tobacco,' a name
since transferred to the plant of which the rolls
were made."

(Such is the case in English; but the Cubans
call cigars *tabaccas* to the present day.)

After leaving Cabaña's, two of us went to visit
the cathedral; but found that we were too late, it
not being open after four p.m. Now, Mr. Trollope's opinion about the exterior of this edifice I
fully concur in, it being, as he says, built of the
very worst materials and in the very worst taste;
but I think he has rather cavalierly dismissed, with

this contemptuous notice, the church beneath
whose chancel lays the body of a man before whose
fame will pale that of many whose ashes rest in
the abbey of Westminster.   I mean that of Christopher Columbus.

Well, not being able to get into the church (for
it can only be called cathedral by courtesy), we
adjourned to the Casa Dominica, the best known
café to strangers to be found in Havana.

The place consists of a large paved courtyard,
with a species of dripping-fountain in the centre, in
whose basin gold fish fed and vegetated.   The
square was surrounded by a covered walk, and a
canvas screen, covering in the whole of the space at
the top, gave a certain appearance like an enclosed
room to the place, and at the same time permitted
a delicious coolness.

Anything was to be got at this establishment—
from sugar plums to gin cocktails—with one exception, they did not make coffee, to our disappointment.   On the opposite side of the way is the
store of this vast refreshment room, and a visit to
the said store afforded us much amusement.

For, in the first place, in the extreme right hand
corner, was a complicated set of machinery driven
by steam, for the manufacture of Guava jelly.
Now, we had often tasted this sweet viscid compound, but had never known before how it was
made.   A description in full would be tiring, but

the main parts of the process were, firstly, crushing
the ripe fruit; then separating the juice from the
rind and pips, and lastly, boiling it in several
copper caldrons, in each of which an agitator,
worked by the engine, was continually revolving till
the juice, as clear as crystal, arrived at the final
pan, and was thence ladled, "all hot," into the
boxes prepared for its reception, big pieces of mem-
brane being previously placed in them. One cannot
imagine a more cleanly mode of preparation, as it is
untouched by hand throughout the whole process.

I cannot say as much for the manufacture of the
preserves—ginger, pine, &c., as, after undergoing
their boiling in syrup, they are turned out by
bucketsful into a large metal-lined box, whence
they are transferred to their bottles and jars
by the not over cleanly hands of the niggers in
attendance.

Yet once more does the black question make its
appearance. But not this time as before, relative
to the respective positions of the free and independent white or black, for in Cuba each man is free
to "wallop his own nigger." The said "wallop-
ing" may not be, and is not, I believe, often inflicted; but the fear of it hangs *in terrorem* over the
woolly heads of the darkies of the island as in other
slave countries. As to my opinions about slavery,
I think (and so I dare say do my readers) that we
may omit them on this occasion, for if I do not

forget, some rather " tall" language, as the Yankees call it, has been already indulged in by me before on this subject. But as this is the first port we have visited where absolute slavery has been both permitted and encouraged by those in authority, it may be amusing to give a literal translation of one or two advertisements which I stumbled across in the daily papers.

" The owner wishes to sell a female black slave, eighteen years of age; also her child, aged three years. The former is warranted free from blemishes, is a good cook, washerwoman, and laundress, and possesses a good temper.

" They may be had either together or separately, but if both are bought together an allowance will be made as discount.—Apply No. — Calle," &c.

" To be sold, a fine negro lad, twenty-one years of age; is accustomed to the care of horses, and is a good house servant. The owner wishes to part with him on account of leaving the island. Freedom from blemishes warranted.—Apply," &c.

Many others to the same effect are to be seen every day in the *Diario* and other papers. Thirty advertisements of this description per diem seemed to me to be about the average.

Next day I went alone to visit the cathedral. It was very difficult to get admittance, as the verger, or party who performed that office, was asleep and would not be roused. However, I was determined to see the inside of it, and at last found a small door open leading to the vestry, through which I passed and entered the church. I was prepared to be very much disappointed—no, that is an Irishism—I mean, to find it not worth looking at, but was, on the contrary, rather pleased. Not that I mean to say that it would take sixth rank among our own first-class churches (excluding cathedrals), but still it was no worse, at all events, than many which I have seen in South America, and which also assume the dignified name of cathedral. In the centre of the chancel is a handsomely gilt pillar supporting a canopy, under which, standing on a globe, is nearly a life-sized image of our Saviour. Some of the pictures seemed good, but as I am no artist it is very possible that my judgment may be worth very little in this respect. But that which I had come to see—the tomb of the great discoverer of America, is, after all, the only object in the church which would repay one for a visit, and me it richly repaid. I have a veneration for the resting-places of the illustrious dead, which I would fain hope is shared by many who may read these pages.

The engraving on the opposite page will convey a better idea than any verbal description of the tomb. It is composed of a yellow slab of marble, worked in bas-relief, let into the wall, on the right

O Restos é Imagen del grande Colon!
Mil siglos duran guardados en la Urna
Yen la remembranza de nuestra Nacion

COLUMBUS' TOMB.   Page 254.

hand side of the chancel, its bottom edge some two
or three feet from the ground. The expression of
the face, of which the drawing, I fear, gives but an
indifferent idea, is extremely sweet ; and if it bears,
as alleged, a close resemblance to the great original,
he must have possessed a countenance which must
have powerfully aided his appeals to Isabella, who
was, I suppose, like the rest of her sex, susceptible
to manly beauty.

And this is the only monument which Spain and
her colony can find taste or means to raise to the
memory of such a man as Christopher Columbus!
Monuments may be useless in themselves, yet they
invite to noble deeds. Had it been France, how
great would have been the difference ; all that art
or money could do to raise a fitting memorial of
such a son would have been done.

As I thought of the vast results which have followed
in the wake of the humble caravel of Columbus, the
more I felt interested in visiting this shrine—for
shrine it is, and should be, to all who have read
with youthful interest the well-known history of
the discovery of the Western Indies, and have
longed to follow in the steps of the great man, and
like him to carve a reputation which shall last so
long as the world endures.

In the evening I accompanied several brother
officers to the opera to hear " Traviata." We all
met at the Casa Dominica, and thence, hiring a

"volante," drove out to the opera house. Every one knows, I suppose, by this time, what a "volante" is. Trollope has so well described this Cuban vehicle, that I will merely say that it is a species of covered gig with the wheels astern of the body; the shafts about eight feet, and not reaching further than the horse's saddle, on top of which sits the driver. Under these circumstances the horse has, one would think, as much to carry and draw as is convenient. I have seen three naval officers in one "volante," and the horse did not seem particularly tired; at all events, *he didn't say so.*

The opera house is a very fair-sized building, and the interior is well fitted up. It is so long since I have seen an English theatre that I can hardly compare it to any, but if I recollect rightly, the Adelphi is about the same size; I may be wrong, however.

"Traviata" is not a favourite piece of mine, so I did not get into ecstasies with the performance. The orchestra seemed good and the singing fair, and that is all I can say about it.

When we reached the landing-place and tried to get a boat, the rascally boatmen wanted an exorbitant fare. However, as there were a good many of us, we reserved our private opinion on that question till we got alongside, and then gave them what we considered a *fair* sum. They growled a good deal, but we were too numerous for them to attempt force, so we went up the side in peace. I heard a

story, however, of an occurrence which took place a
day or two before our arrival, which will serve to
illustrate the sort of fraternity composing the water-
men of Havana.

An American gentleman, the captain of a large
ship lying in the harbour, was one night anxious
to get on board. Having a large quantity of money
in doubloons about him, he thought it prudent to
affect no knowledge of Spanish (though he spoke it
perfectly), hoping that if any rascality was intended,
they might, being unsuspicious of his comprehend-
ing them, make some remarks aloud which would
put him on his guard.

His prudence was rewarded. When they were
a few hundred yards from the landing-place, one
proposed to the other to rob and murder their pas-
senger, being aware of the money on his person, as
he had seen him receive it a short time previously.
Quietly but quickly the captain cocked the small
revolver in his breast pocket, and when, after a few
more words, one of them laid his oar in and stepped
aft with the intention of stabbing him, a discharge
from the pistol stopped his course, and he fell dead
in the bottom of the boat. The other ruffian now
attempted to grapple the American, but a second
bullet disposed of him as effectually as the other.

The captain was now in an unpleasant predica-
ment. Two dead bodies, when alone in a boat, are
disagreeable companions; and besides that, one pair

of arms could hardly manage her. However, he contrived to pull the boat back to the wharf, and then, obtaining police assistance, had the bodies carried up to the police office, while he followed them, and reported his adventure to the superintendent.

Fortunately for him they were both recognised as notorious scoundrels, and, his story being believed, he was allowed to go at large without further inquiry. But, somehow, he did not care to go ashore much more in Havana; or, at all events, to come off by himself at night.

I was assured that this kind of attempt had been frequently made. Anyhow, *we* took good care to come off in parties of three and four, or more.

The day after the opera night, the Deputy Captain-General of Cuba came off, with a numerous suite, to visit the Prince. There is, I believe, a law which forbids the Captain-General himself to go afloat; so he sent his deputy. The uniforms worn by these officers were certainly good specimens in the way of variety, for every combination of colour to be found in the uniforms of civilized nations was there. There was blue covered with gold, and gold, apparently, turned up with blue,—so profuse was the amount of the yellow ornament visible. Red, green, &c., &c., each had representatives. I overheard one marine say to another. "I say, Jim, they kivies beats them what we saw at the *uproar* (Anglicé—opera); don't 'em?" to which "Jim" replied, "There be a heap of gowld on them, surely; but where do ut all come from?"

His Royal Highness Prince Alfred paid a visit to the Captain-General before we left. The aides de camp, and others present at the interview, were profoundly astonished at the Prince's affability—so, at least, they told us. Their own princes, they said, never deigned to notice in any way those who were not of royal blood, or the very highest nobility. Altogether his visit produced a most favourable impression on the minds of the Cubans.

About eleven, a.m., the same day R——, H——, and myself went on shore ; the two former for the purpose of purchasing a very handy kind of pistol —an American invention—of which a great many were exposed for sale in the stalls, which abound under the numerous arcades which Havana rejoices in. The vendor told H—— to try the effect of a shot on a box at the back of his store ; which H—— accordingly did. The bullet went through the wood and evidently made a commotion inside. On asking what were the contents of the box, the owner quietly replied, " Crackers."

On our return to the ship we found things in a commotion. A squall coming on suddenly, had caused us to drag our anchor until we fouled an American brigantine and slightly damaged her. The estimate made by her master of the cost of repairing the mischief, and that made by our carpenter, were "horses of different colours" entirely. We did not, however, remain long enough at the Havana to learn how the case was ultimately settled.

On the 27th January, 1862, we left for Bermuda, at which anchorage we arrived on the 4th February, 1862.

CHAPTER XVII.

THE *St. George* had been at anchor but a very few
hours when the news flew through the ship that
we were ordered home. It is astonishing how
quickly any yarn, which interests the crew in
general, flies about the decks of a man-of-war. On
the present occasion electricity was nothing to it;
for the intelligence seemed to have reached the
quarter deck, the cook's galley, and the fore cockpit simultaneously.

We had not been so very long absent from our
own shores that any among us suffered particularly
from home sickness; but we in the gun-room were
glad enough—always bearing in mind, nevertheless, the sad cause of our hasty departure from the
station.

So one fine day, the 7th February, we steamed
out of the coral-girt Bermudas, and proceeded on
our homeward way rejoicing.

But the *St. George* is a peculiar ship. The clerk

of the weather must have been omitted at the invitations given when she was launched, and shows that he has never forgotten the slight by always serving out to us the worst weather which at any particular moment the great brewhouse of nature may be manufacturing.

On our passage home he let us have it with a vengeance. The two former gales (which have been already described at some length) faded into insignificance compared to the one which we now encountered. Naval men are accused of a weakness for always considering the last gale they may happen to be in as the worst they have ever met. Perhaps this accusation has some foundation in fact; but, at all events, on this particular occasion we had, I fancy, good reasons for our verdict, that it "were worser nor any we had ever sailed in before," as an old quartermaster phrased it. For in addition to the personal discomforts which our previous experience had taught us were inevitable when the "winds blew and the waves arose," the much vexed ocean left traces on our outside (let alone the inside of the ship), which amply proved that our accounts of it on reaching home were not unfounded on fact.

In the first place, two of our quarter boats were *blown* away; that is to say, they were blown inboard on the mizen rigging, and the waves, aided by our own hatchets, completed what the wind had begun, for so total was the smash, that it would have been as useless as impossible to have attempted to save them.

But that, bad as it was, did not immediately affect our creature comforts within-board; but just fancy to yourself, reader, that you are seated comfortably (barring a very lively motion) in your study or parlour, engaged in reading, drawing, or some other interesting amusement—and then imagine your feelings should you behold a mighty mass of waters rush in at your windows, smashing them to atoms by the blow, and then hurry away in its relentless strength your chest of drawers, your bureau, your bed, nay, the very walls themselves, until the rooms on the other floor became as one mighty pond of some two feet in depth, which, rushing hither and thither in its newly found bed, should reduce all that was spoilable to one general mass of sea-salted pulp.

If your imagination is sufficiently lively for this, you will then be able to realize to yourself the events of a certain five minutes during the gale, when the Commander's cabin was thus treated.

The sort of feeling expressed by the sea-sick and repentant marine, who "sold his farm to come to sea," was precisely our own during this passage. Many were the declarations made by various parties that no earthly power should again tempt them to brave the dangers of the sea—all to be forgotten when smooth water and pleasant breezes should again prevail. And so it is with many other intentions in this world, far more serious than the one in question!

As we neared the English coast our opportunities of taking observations became rare, and our position, after three days without taking them, would have been but for soundings very uncertain. As the weather clerk was determined that we should not fetch Plymouth, and is moreover one with whom arguing is perfectly useless, it was deemed advisable to bear up for Cork, or rather Queenstown, at which latter harbour we arrived on the 3rd of March, 1862.

H.R.H. Prince Alfred and Major Cowell, R.E., left the ship, *en route* to Osborne, shortly after we anchored; and here, as far as they are concerned, any further notice of their movements in this book terminates.

We left Queenstown after a short stay, and again tried to reach Plymouth. But the fates were still unpropitious, and the *St. George* was obliged to seek refuge from the heavy easterly gale in Scilly.

The pilots who boarded us gave us sad accounts of the damage done by the gale, and congratulated us on being comfortably anchored, instead of being exposed to its fury.

When it had somewhat moderated we left Scilly, and finally anchored within the protecting breakwater at Plymouth on the 7th March, 1862.

Here I conclude this imperfect account of our wanderings, and would fain hope that, even if not interesting to the public at large, the foregoing pages will recall many a pleasant hour and many a beautiful scene to the minds of those who have been my fellow-shipmates, to whom I wish most unfeignedly all happiness here and hereafter.

BIBLIOLIFE

Old Books Deserve a New Life
www.bibliolife.com

Did you know that you can get most of our titles in our trademark **EasyScript**™ print format? **EasyScript**™ provides readers with a larger than average typeface, for a reading experience that's easier on the eyes.

Did you know that we have an ever-growing collection of books in many languages?

Order online:
www.bibliolife.com/store

Or to exclusively browse our **EasyScript**™ collection:
www.bibliogrande.com

At BiblioLife, we aim to make knowledge more accessible by making thousands of titles available to you – quickly and affordably.

Contact us:
BiblioLife
PO Box 21206
Charleston, SC 29413

LIST OF PLACES VISITED BY H.M.S. *ST. GEORGE*,
WITH DATES OF ARRIVAL AND DEPARTURE.

Name of Place.	Date of Arrival.	Date of Departure.
PLYMOUTH—Sound	... ...	January 16, 1861
BARBADOES—Carlisle Bay . .	February 21, 1861	March 1, ,,
ST. VINCENT—Kingston Bay .	March 2, ,,	,, 4, ,,
Do. —Walliban Bay .	,, 4, ,,	,, 4, ,,
ST. LUCIA—Port Castries . .	,, 5, ,,	,, 7, ,,
MARTINIQUE—Fort Royal . .	,, 7, ,,	,, 9, ,,
Do. —St. Pierre . .	,, 9, ,,	,, 10, ,,
DOMINICA—Roseau Roads . .	,, 10, ,,	,, 12, ,,
GUADALOUPE—Basseterre . .	,, 12, ,,	,, 14, ,,
ANTIGUA—St. John's . .	,, 14, ,,	,, 18, ,,
MONTSERRAT—Plymouth Bay .	,, 18, ,,	,, 19, ,,
NEVIS—Charlestown . . .	,, 19, ,,	,, 20, ,,
ST. CHRISTOPHER—Basseterre .	,, 20, ,,	,, 22, ,,
TORTOLA—Rondtown . . .	,, 24, ,,	,, 25, ,,
ST. THOMAS—	,, 25, ,,	,, 27, ,,
SANTA CRUZ—Frederickstadt .	,, 28, ,,	,, 29, ,,
JAMAICA—Port Royal . . .	April 2, ,,	April 10, ,,
GT. INAGNA—Man-of-War Bay	,, 16, ,,	,, 17, ,,
LONG ISLAND—	,, 18, ,,	,, 23, ,,
BERMUDA—Ireland Island . .	May 2, ,,	May 15, ,,
NOVA SCOTIA—Halifax . .	,, 22, ,,	June 22, ,,
MADAME ISLAND—Arichat . .	June 24, ,,	,, 29, ,,
CAPE BRETON ISLAND—Louisberg	,, 29, ,,	July 3, ,,
Do. —S. Sydney	July 3, ,,	,, 8, ,,
Do. —N. Sydney	,, 8, ,,	,, 9, ,,
Do. —Port Hood	,, 11, ,,	,, 13, ,,
PRINCE EDWARD'S ISLAND — Hillsboro' Bay	,, 13, ,,	,, 16, ,,
NOVA SCOTIA—Pictou . . .	,, 16, ,,	,, 18, ,,
CAPE BRETON—Habitan's Bay.	,, 18, ,,	,, 19, ,,
NOVA SCOTIA—Halifax . . .	,, 23, ,,	October 18, ,,

Proceeded up Bedford Basin on 21st September ; returned to Halifax Harbour 27th September.

NOVA SCOTIA—Ship Harbour for Tangier	October 18, 1861	October 21, 1861
CAPE BRETON ISLAND—S. Sydney	,, 22, ,,	,, 24, ,,
Do. —N. Sydney	,, 24, ,,	,, 25, ,,
Do. —Louisberg	,, 25, ,,	,, 26, ,,

Name of Place.	Date of Arrival.	Date of Departure.
MADAME ISLAND—Arichat . .	October 26, 1861	October 30, 1861
NOVA SCOTIA—Halifax . . .	,, 31, ,,	November 19, ,,
NEW PROVIDENCE, BAHAMAS— Nassau	December 2, ,,	December 4, ,,
ABACO ISLAND—S.W. Bay . .	,, 4, ,,	,, 6, ,,
NEW PROVIDENCE—S.W. Bay .	,, 6, ,,	,, 9, ,,
MANGUANA—S.W. Bay . . .	,, 17, ,,	,, 19, ,,
JAMAICA—Port Royal . . .	,, 21, ,,	,, 25, ,,
Cruising off Cape San Antonio	,, 29, ,,	January 1, 1862
MEXICO—Sacraficios	January 6, 1862	,, 8, ,,
Do. —Anton Lizardo . .	,, 8, ,,	,, 17, ,,,
Do. —Vera Cruz . . .	,, 17, ,,	,, 17, ,,
CUBA—Havana	,, 22, ,,	,, 27, ,,
BERMUDA—Ireland Island . .	February 4, ,,	February 7, ,,
CORK—Queenstown	March 3, ,,	... ...

FINIS.

9 781103 472871